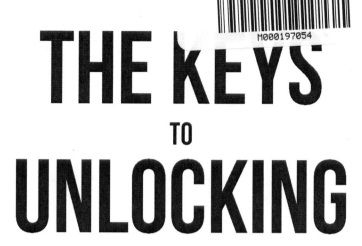

THE KEYS
TO
UNLOCKING
YOUR
Joy

Cathy
Thank you so
much for being
a big part of
my journey
Jaiya C.

JAIYA CLARKE

ELOHAI
INTERNATIONAL
PUBLISHING & MEDIA

Reviews for *Keys to Unlocking Your Joy*

"You know those books you buy ten copies of and forcefully give to everyone you know because it's that good? Yeah, this is one of those books. What a timely message! My friend and mentor Jaiya Clarke does a beautiful job at taking your hand and leading you to those beautiful places in your heart that are desperately waiting to be filled with joy. This book engages the reader with biblically sound truths that I believe will challenge, bless, and empower all of those who read it."

—Avanta T., San Diego, CA

"So many nuggets in here! Thank you for being obedient and allowing God to shine through you. This book is going to break strongholds and free so many people from bondage. A relationship with Him and His joy is so filling and I'm glad you're helping people to recognize this. You definitely embody the joy of the Lord, so this book is so fitting."

—Monique F., San Diego, CA

"This book is amazing! I was drawn in after just a few minutes into the Introduction. I enjoyed how you speak on your faith walk and give us tips to make time for God: study His word and how it will change our lives."

—Anjie S., San Diego, CA

"Congratulations Jaiya!! I'm super proud of you! It takes a certain level of courage and tenacity to write and publish such a personal book. This book invites the world into the vulnerable spaces of her personal life experience as she opens it up to the world. Now that is bold! As a reader, I love to read and feel the personality and characteristics of the author and you gave us just that. Many times throughout the book, I felt as though we were sitting in a room having one those 'good ole girl talks' about life as we normally do. *The Keys to Unlocking Your Joy* by Jaiya Clarke is simply a MASTERPIECE."

—Demetricia C., Ft. Lauderdale, FL

"I have been puzzled on how to find consistent joy in life. Reading this book has opened my eyes to bettering my relationship with God and creating healthy habits while centering God. Jaiya did an excellent job providing facts and breaking down the "keys" to gain thorough understanding and insight. The prayers throughout the book provided me with guidance and showed me how to simplistically pray and that praying is to not only ask for material things or for situations to be better, but to give thanks and to ask for guidance. Overall, this book has inspired consistency and kindness. Consistency within my life, my relationships, and especially within my faith. Kindness was inspired by acknowledging how setting scheduled appointments to check in with God is a practice of self-care and self-kindness. Great read. I'm recommending this book, hands down!"

—Maya E-T., La Mesa, CA

"Joy comes in the morning and peace comes in the morning, let me hear you sing! The unwavering and overflowing fountain of joy we all seek comes from God. To commune with Him is to experience authentic joy. *The Keys to Unlocking Your Joy* outlines scriptures, group readings, comprehensive questions, and sweet prayers aligned with God, our true source. As you read this book, you will master such keys within to keep winning. No matter how unhappy our circumstances may seem, in Him, we can remain joyful."

—Rachel D., San Diego, CA

"Jaiya reveals the truth about obtaining true, unfiltered joy and happiness in your life. She gives you easy to understand, relatable tools that can be used daily in your walk with Christ, no matter if you're new in your walk or seasoned. Life isn't a walk in the park, but if your heart is yearning to obtain true joy that will stay consistent even when your faith is tested or you feel like all hope is lost, Jaiya will walk you through the steps in obtaining the keys to unlocking your joy!"

—Brittan S., San Diego, CA

Published by ELOHAI International Publishing & Media
P.O. Box 1883
Cypress, Texas 77410
www.ElohaiPublishing.com

ISBN: 978-1-953535-47-4

Printed in the United States of America

DEDICATION

This book is dedicated to all of my brothers and sisters in Christ
who desire a non-negotiable relationship with the author
of our life story and the creator of our everlasting joy.
The one true living God.

To my parents, Mr. and Mrs. Keys, this book is your legacy.

FOREWORD

When I heard the scripture, "Seek ye first the kingdom of God and all of His righteousness...," it sounded like a simple enough thing to do. When I read it for myself, it seemed to imply a lot more. Later in life, the same passage seemed to say, "YOU first seek." Later still, the scripture spoke to me of individual responsibility, deeper levels and "inside work." Before my daughter became a Clarke her last name was Keys. Jaiya Keys. Jaiya has always had a creative side, an ability to see a different view of people, places, and things. Jaiya was a child to wonder about more of life's "what ifs". As a child she was a visionary. I remember going to places and within minutes Jaiya would have reorganized and redesigned the entire room! Jaiya would also draw elaborate storytelling pictures and fashion. Always creating, always finding joy in the simple things. This book definitely continues along that vein. She continues to guide us toward our individual responsibility of intentionally connecting to God as well as how to unlock more joyous journeys. As the reader you will receive an exclusive gift of the wisdom that she pours into me during our mother-daughter talks. Congratulations, Jaiya!

Love Mom,

Irma Keys

TABLE OF CONTENTS

INTRODUCTION

Before we begin, I must first share with you two of my favorite scriptures:

1) "The thief comes only in order to steal and kill and destroy. I came that they may have and enjoy life, and have it in abundance [to the full, till it overflows]." John 10:10 AMP

2) "Joyful is the person who finds wisdom, the one who gains understanding. For wisdom is more profitable than silver and her wages are better than gold." Proverbs 3:13 NLT

First, can we just pause and put a hand of praise in the air because the Bible literally references "wisdom" as a woman? Ok, now let's proceed to the goodness!

Did you know that it is very common to be unhappy? People are becoming unhappier and unhappier by the minute. We allow the tiniest life adjustment to make us totally tank emotionally. We live in a world with so many challenges and many obstacles. We also live in a world where many people have mastered the skill to consecutively WIN at life by mastering the keys to joy. To master the keys to joy, you must understand what joy is—surprisingly, not many people do.

Joy is defined as a feeling of great pleasure and happiness. Joy is also a cheerful and vibrant happiness. The full spiritual meaning of Joy is when Gods goodness is outwardly expressed. Most people believe happiness is something they either have to "find" or "go get." Another common belief is that our happiness

1

is attached to another human being, such as our children, family, friends, or significant others. Granted, you may have to move around a little bit and make a few adjustments to your relationships as you begin to understand what brings you happiness and joy. The truth is our happiness is within us every day, just waiting to be released. That's right! Your happiness and joy are on standby, waiting for you to choose to let go of anger, forgive the pain of your past, and confront your fears. Are you ready to do the homework and get it done?

The dictionary describes happiness as a mental or emotional state of well-being defined by positive or pleasant emotions ranging from contentment to intense joy. Who else wants some of that "intense joy?" **raises hand** Unlocking our joy does not mean we are free from experiencing moments of unhappiness, sadness, suffering or disappointment; those moments will trickle in from time to time. When we learn how to unlock our happiness and joy, we are mastering the ability to defeat toxic emotions, such as doubt, fear, insecurity, rejection, hurt, anxiety, depression, and shame, to name a few.

When we begin to pay attention to life, we notice that God has been with us all along. We notice the sounds we hear, the sights we see, where we are, our surroundings, the words people say, their facial expressions when they speak, and what they mean. We become aware of someone's intentions and their body language. Then we will not be anxious or afraid but thankful that God has gifted us to see beyond what we can see with our natural eyes and unlock the truth. Awareness can unlock so many doors to opportunity. These signals help us determine what and who is creating toxic experiences in our lives and what brings us joy and peace.

In this book, you will unlock the secrets to accomplishing your heart's desires, understanding your identity in Christ, loving yourself first, and releasing and attracting love from others. People who think that money equals success and happiness couldn't have it more wrong. The Bible speaks of a man named Simon who had all the riches in the world except the gifts of the

Holy Spirit. He literally wanted to buy his way into a relationship with God. Well, that didn't turn out so good, and you can read what happens to that guy in Acts chapter 8.

Somewhere down the line, we've learned how to pray to God as if he responds like a genie in a bottle—as if we can hand over our shopping lists of needs or request drive-through blessings, super-sized, of course, with a side of grace. Question, who is serving who? In the Gospels, Jesus teaches about kingdom and not church. People who are intentionally pursuing deeper levels of who God has called them to be prioritize relationship over religion. Our relationship with God is an opportunity for our soul to breathe and our spirit to blossom. Studying and understanding the mystery and history of the Bible is the key to unlocking an entire kingdom ready to be revealed through our relationship with God.

Our relationship with God is beyond surface-level connections like visiting a building once a week. Our Bible asks us to become the church, but how? Money can bring wealth, but the true meaning of success is happiness and joy! Yes, joy! When we reach our desired level in life, we must know the keys to maintaining that level, and we must know how to increase it to the next level. It is very possible to have double doses of joy every day, but we must unlock it with intention!

In this book, you will learn how to unlock happiness and joy in your relationships, your body, your finances, your personal growth, and most importantly, in spirit. You will learn the keys to the power of shifting your perception from negative to positive within seconds. I wouldn't be too surprised (and I hope that you wouldn't be either) if you unlock your calling after completing this book! God is waiting for us to spiritually wake up to our purpose and inheritance. "Rise up, daughters of the Most High God. Rise up!" You are getting ready to discover the *Keys to Unlocking Your Joy.*

Thank you so much for picking up this book. I hope you are ready to dive in and enjoy!

Master Key

"When the righteous cry for help, the Lord hears and delivers them out of all their troubles. The Lord is near to the brokenhearted and saves the crushed in spirit. Many are the afflictions of the righteous, but the Lord delivers him out of them all."

~ *Psalm 34:17-19 ESV*

Chapter One

CONNECTING TO CHRIST

God is the Source

This walk is a faith walk. When I think about connecting to Christ, I think about how electricity in a light bulb works. A light bulb is just a piece of glass on its own, but when connected to its power source, it has the power to light up an entire room. When we do an act of faith, such as worship, prayer, or Bible study, we begin to illuminate, and the same thing happens to us. This illumination is undeniably magnetic as it draws people from all walks of life interested in the source of our brightness. There's just something about you! Have you heard that before? Of course, you have. The calling on your life is the key to being an influencer to the influencer. You have a light about you, a glow, and a sparkle. It's the charge that you receive when you receive confidence and confirmation from the most excellent power source, God.

There are many ways to get plugged into God. One way is by simply talking to him. You can't worry about what it looks like; you just have to decide to begin. Back when I was seeking

God and growing in my faith, I talked to God out loud (in a quiet space) or wrote out the good, bad, and the ugly as a daily letter to God or daily debrief meeting. As a wife and a mother, I find myself still doing this. My relationship with God began as a friendship. Jesus Christ is the perfect friend. I can count on his unfailing love, compassion, presence, and protection even when my other friends are busy tackling their own issues.

When I suddenly lost my father to a heart attack as a young adult, my relationship with God continued to grow. It then progressed to the role of a father to a child. When we come into this world, we all have a natural father, but when we choose to follow the teachings of Jesus Christ, we become God's adopted children. That's a pretty big deal! It was always our destiny to be chosen by God and adopted by him, the creator of this whole world, *"even as he chose us in him before the foundation of the world, that we should be holy and blameless before him. In love he predestined us for adoption to himself as sons through Jesus Christ, according to the purpose of his will, to the praise of his glorious grace, with which he has blessed us in the Beloved"* ~ *Ephesians 1:4-6 ESV*.

Once I decided to practice having a relationship with God, I realized the best way to do this was to follow the blueprint, a.k.a. user's manual, that already had a successful and consistent track record.

As we open our user's manual and learn more about living life in an abundant way, we understand that the Bible is more than just a book written over 2,000 years ago. It's a user's manual that provides step-by-step instructions on how to be successful in all relationships—relationships with family, friends, children, coworkers, significant others, and even our enemies.

When I chose Christianity, in addition to establishing a relationship with God, it seemed to unlock a new level in my life. Getting plugged in with other believers is the key that unlocks spiritual growth. Connecting to Christ is an amazing spiritual journey. I connected to a group of people who understood that we are all on this earth to defeat one enemy, shine a light on darkness with the truth, and fill the world with as much good as possible. They believe and follow God's plan as it has been laid out for us by his Son, Jesus Christ. These people have a similar desire to grow and become better by walking out their faith, overcoming their obstacles, and becoming better daily. The only way to plug into God's ultimate radiance and brightness is to follow Jesus Christ. Our relationship with the one true living God is the key to the abundance of joy and happiness.

The User's Manual

With billions of copies sold every year, the Bible is the most-read book in the world and has continued to exceed the bestseller list for over fifty years. By demand, the Bible has been translated into more than 3,000 international languages. Many people have a Bible, but our lives progressively transform only when we understand how to use this big, powerful book filled with hidden mysteries and prolific history. This book is the compass on our journey, the blueprint of our life's development, and the open book for the tests we must overcome daily.

The English Bible has sixty-six books divided into two main parts, the Old Testament and the New Testament. The Old Testament contains essential scriptures of the Jewish faith, while the New Testament allows us to see God live out life in human form (as Jesus Christ). The New Testament is the fulfillment of the prophesies we read about in the Old Testament. All things become possible if done by God's design instead of our own. When we follow the teachings of Jesus Christ, we can use both the Old Testament and the New Testament. The Old Testament is where God spoke through many prophets about his plans for the world, and the New Testament is where God spoke through his son Jesus Christ.

When I began studying the Bible and establishing a relationship with Christ, my biggest question was what would happen if I was disobedient. I was a "spicy" little girl, and my favorite response was always, "But why, though?" Everything is questionable and worth a proper discussion before you get my agreement. My husband calls this habit "trust but verify." God knows this about his daughter and swiftly responded to my inquiry about the repercussions of my disobedience as follows:

> *"But if you will not obey the voice of the Lord your God or be careful to do all his commandments and his statutes that I command you today, then all these curses shall come upon you and overtake you. Cursed shall you be in the city and cursed shall you be in the field. Cursed shall be your basket and your kneading bowl. Cursed shall be the fruit of your womb and the fruit of your ground, the increase of your herds and the young of your flock. Cursed shall you be when you come in, and cursed shall you be when you go out.*
>
> *"The Lord will send on you curses, confusion, and frustration in all that you undertake to do, until you are destroyed and perish quickly on account of the evil of your deeds, because you have forsaken me."*
>
> *~ Deuteronomy 28:15-20 ESV*

I don't know about you, but after reading the word "cursed" over five times on one page, I decided I didn't want a seat at the table of the cursed. I realized my decision to use the blueprint in God's Word was pretty solid. Next, I read the Gospels, a.k.a. "the good news," which consists of Matthew, Mark, Luke, and John. These books are so dope collectively that I couldn't tell you which one I enjoy reading the most. In the Gospels, we hear different perspectives of Jesus' plan for a kingdom life shared through the eyes of people who had a direct relationship with Jesus. In this section of the Bible, we learn the most about Jesus Christ. We learn about his miracles and how we can put the teachings of each book into action to fulfill God's plan. In the Gospels, we have the key to unlock our biggest questions like "Who is Jesus?" "Who is God?" and "Who is The Holy Spirit?"

The Gospels also tell one of the world's most famous sto-ries—the resurrection of Jesus Christ. This is the amazing story of how the Son of God was nailed to a cross, declared dead, buried in a tomb, and walked out of his grave alive and well. I get excited when God shows off, with *HIS* fancy self! We know this is a confirmed event because Jewish, Roman, and Christian histories all confirm that Jesus Christ was killed on a cross. As a documented part of history, we know the information is not pla-giarized. Historians also have documented the disciples' various experiences of Jesus Christ after his death.

"There is, as far as I am aware, no prima facie evidence that the death and resurrection of Jesus is a mythological construct, drawing on myths and rites of the dying and rising of gods of the surrounding world. While studied with profit against the background of Jewish resurrection belief, the faith in the death and resurrection of Jesus re-tains its unique character in the history of religions."
~ Tryggve Mettinger, The Riddle of Resurrection:
Dying and Rising Gods in the Ancient Near East,
2001, pg. 221

Let's Pray:

Heavenly Father, today I'm seeking a deeper relationship with you. I invite you into my life to remove areas that distract me. Holy Spirit, I invite you to guide me into an obedient walk with you. Lord, design an abundant life for me full of your blessings and void of curses. Create a new level of awareness in me as I read and understand your written Word. Create an awakening in my spirit that desires more of you daily.

In Jesus' name, amen.

Master Key

"But seek first the kingdom of God and his righteousness, and all these things will be added to you."

~ *Matthew 6:33 ESV*

Chapter Two

PUT GOD FIRST

Scheduling Daily Appointments

Establishing a relationship with Jesus Christ is above the routine systems of "being a Christian." "Being a Christian" is doing all of the outward things instead of focusing on the transformation and renewal of our mind, heart, and soul. We get into a ritual habit of going to Sunday worship, weekly Bible study, small groups, and youth ministry activities. We can't leave out our service and volunteering. While I believe in doing these things as a part of the spiritual growth process, scheduling time with God daily is a priority. It keeps us from becoming overwhelmed and feeling like overcooked Christians—doing all the work without proper instructions from God.

In my journey for a relationship with God, I have grown to love the book of Deuteronomy because I am a lover of truth, integrity, and intention. Deuteronomy is filled with God's promises to the followers of Jesus Christ—promises that never return void. Over the years, I have had the opportunity to test the theory of obedience = blessings, and yes, it's true! There has not been a moment in my life when I have stepped out on biblical wisdom, insight, and faith and didn't come back with a blessing receipt. It's been a wild ride—trust me. We have receipts of God's promises in our marriages, our parenting, and our career passions. We even have receipts of God wanting to show out and bless us just because. The only way to keep track of the receipts is to document them and refer to them as evidence that we have a reciprocal relationship with a living God.

The beginning of every relationship starts out awkward. We don't know who should speak first, and we don't want to look weird doing so. Spending time with God and reading his Word awakens an interest in our spirit. God wants all the T.E.A. (thoughts, emotions, and apprehensions)! I'm not talking about gossip; I'm talking about going straight to the source for strategy training. What better than to share life situations with someone who can actually do something about it? God wants to hear directly from us so he can help us with a strategy. He wants to inspire us to create, develop an interest to discover our calling, and desire to be a better human being. We can open our Bible to any page, and just one sentence may be enough to encourage us for the entire day! I find the "Sword of the Spirit," also known as our Bible, is fascinating, vibrant, alive, and so much better than binging Netflix.

Everyone's schedule is different, so decide the best time of day to spend some quiet time with God and commit to it. Make sure it's a time when you are alert and fully plugged in. Our relationship with God is an exchange—we want to hear from God, and he wants to hear from us. We must be awake and aware during our time with God. Most people try to talk to God first, so early in the morning between 4 a.m. and 7 a.m. is ideal, but not mandatory. Once you commit to a time during the day, intentionally create reoccurring appointments to train your body to develop the habit of scheduling and sticking to your daily appointments with God. Remember, the God we serve loves walk-in appointments, too, so if your schedule is booked, don't beat yourself up about it. Check in with God as soon as you have time and watch how your day shifts.

Meeting Minutes

We want to hear from God, and God wants to hear from us. We may begin to see all kinds of things clearer and hear random words being whispered directly into our ears. Documenting these words, sights, and sounds becomes essential for us to refer to in various situations. God is always ahead of any issue that might show up in our lives, and he gives us all kinds of signs and signals before any event or conversation. Journaling is a smart way to keep the minutes of your meetings with God. Journaling allows us to document what God is specifically saying to us. It helps us realize the current challenges we are facing and how we plan to be more obedient to God. Journaling also highlights the help we need to intentionally execute these plans.

Once we have processed all the thoughts sitting in our spirit and put them on paper, we now have something we can refer to when someone we love faces a similar issue. I speak a lot about receipts from our exchanges with God. It's crucial to document where and how God has shown up in our lives. When we document our encounters with God, we have tangible proof that God is alive and working in our lives. Documenting our receipts allows us to see our faith in action. The more we have faith that God always shows up, the more we will trust in him to provide everything we need.

Prayer and Bible Study

Taking just thirty seconds out of your day to listen to the audio Bible while you make up your bed or make your coffee is transforming. As a mother always in a time crunch, I've always found peace after my daily appointments with God. The Bible tells us that when we read the Bible, we can expect proper training in areas where we need further discipline. It has the power to correct and reset lingering bad habits, and will also equip us to teach these things to our family and friends in a clear and relatable way. We can find this confirmation in 2 Timothy: *"All Scripture is breathed out by God and profitable for teaching, for reproof, for correction, and for training in righteousness, that the man of God may be complete, equipped for every good work."* ~ *2 Timothy 3:16-17 ESV*

Do you have a Bible? Selecting one that you understand is an important key to intentional and effective Bible study. I recommend a study Bible—preferably one that includes a map and commentary. Lately, my Bible study has graduated to a Holy Spirit-led experience. In the morning when I wake up, I say, "Ok, Lord, which book do you have me in today?" By putting that question into the atmosphere, my spirit is quickened. As I open my Bible to that particular book, I flip through pages and read the section titles to see if anything resonates with my current situation. Suddenly, boom! A word from God is highlighted, and I dive into Bible study. This method came after years of trusting the Lord to be the wonderful counselor the Bible mentions in Isaiah 9:6.

The SOAP Bible study model is a great way to begin. SOAP is an acronym for scripture, observation, application, and prayer. An important key to putting God first is committing to the habit and creating a routine that you can stick to. The "S" in SOAP is for scripture. Once we decide on a Bible book, we need to choose a chapter and read it multiple times. Then we can read it and look up the chapter in different Bible versions. Biblegateway.com is a great way to quickly access different versions. Playing the passage in an audio Bible is helpful as well.

The "O" in SOAP stands for observation. I'm using Esther chapter 1 as an example. Immediately, we discover that the Book of Esther takes place in the regions between India and Ethiopia. With this information, we can pull out our map to explore what that area would look like today. What ethnicities are there? Does this area still exist, or has it been overthrown by another nation? When you do an internet search for that region, is the land like a desert? Is it beachy? Full of water and palm trees? Or is it a thriving city?

Once you have read the scripture a few times, choose the parts that stood out to you and write them down. Writing naturally wires the information to our brain vs. typing or texting. After you have written out the scripture, personalize it. Make it your own by putting yourself in the shoes of the character. How would you handle things if you were in Esther or Queen Vashti's shoes? Rewriting the experience as if it is happening to you is key to remembering what you just studied.

After observing the passage, it's time to apply what we just read. Application is the "A" in SOAP. Bibles aren't cheap! What's the point of owning a fancy user's manual if we don't use the tools in it? If we believe that all scripture is breathed out by the Holy Spirit as it says in 2 Timothy 3:16-17, then it's time to say, "Ok, God, I see what you did there. What are you trying to tell me?" And begin thinking about how you can apply what you just read to your life. Does the passage give you something to put into action today?

Finally, the "P" in SOAP stands for prayer. Beginning and ending Bible study with prayer invites God into your understanding. It is the key that unlocks the wisdom and knowledge that is often hidden in the Word of God. Prayer is just a form of meditation that allows us to continuously think about what we have read.

As we read in our Bible, we also understand that if we start our day and our decisions with God, our to-do list will create itself. When we discuss our plans with God first and wait just five seconds longer for him to respond, we will have more confidence about our next move.

In our Bible, we also read that God is everywhere and that we should love him with every area of our heart. Some areas in my heart are my husband, my daughter, my parents, and my personal and professional relationships. Before I can pour into those areas, I must love and seek him first. After that, everything flows. *"And he said to him. "You shall love the Lord your God with all your heart and with all your soul and with all your mind. This is the great and first commandment."* ~Matthew 22:37-38 ESV

Every Minute Counts

Putting God first provides us with guidance, direction, and a clear understanding of what steps we should take in real time. Praying before we act on our thoughts or emotions also allows us to receive answers that may deposit words of life into others. As Christians, we will always be tested; thankfully, we have a relationship with a Father who has left us a book of answers. So, in essence, someone walking in a relationship with Christ is walking with an open book test!

Recently I've even been testing the theory of putting God first as it relates to my body. I was in my car one day battling with a headache. Usually, headaches aren't my thing, but that day, this headache was just being a pest. I closed my eyes and began to pray, asking God to handle the pain. I also began to say the name of Jesus while praying, and then I took it a little deeper and started declaring God as my healer (Jehovah Rapha). In less than thirty seconds, that headache was gone. In my car, I silently talked to God about my pain. There were no tears, I didn't have worship music on, and I wasn't shouting at God about what I was going through. It was just a simple silent conversation with my Father, the healer.

Once I decided to allow God to work on my pain, it ended. This practice must be used in every area of our daily lives, starting with our hair follicles all the way down to the very creases at the bottom of our feet. Great is our Lord.

Take some time each day to intentionally connect to Christ. Consider what is the best time and stick to it as much as possible. Also, give yourself some grace if you miss your scheduled appointment with God. Things happen. We serve a God who is overjoyed when we acknowledge him and give him thanks any time of the day.

Pray with me,

Wonderful Father, we thank you for choosing us over and over again. Help us to place your name in every area of our lives. We identify your name, Jesus, above all darkness, uncertainty, and pain. Remind us that transformation and growth begin with you so that we can store this truth in our hearts. Today, we give you full authority to build our lives. You are our wonderful counselor, a mighty God, an everlasting Father, and the Prince of Peace. Hold our hands as we let go of fear, doubt, and control to walk with you.

In Jesus' name, amen.

"By faith we understand that the universe was formed at God's command, so that what is seen was not made out of what was visible."

~ *Hebrews 11:3 ESV*

Chapter Three

KINGDOM TECHNOLOGY

Unseen Battles and Aerial Warfare

Did you know that we have access to top-secret intelligence that the enemy wants? We enter the fight only when we release the knowledge God has downloaded into our spirit. Our dreams and spiritual downloads are innovative "kingdom technology." We are an exclusive group of people who receive one-on-one top-secret training from God, which the enemy does not have access to. It's so important to identify and execute all the freely available tools we need to win the battles of life. In this chapter, we will talk about a few ways to do this.

We begin this training by taking a spiritual gifts test online to identify the gifts that we naturally access the most and those we need to strengthen. Spiritual gifts tests are like any other personality test. They gauge how we naturally respond to circumstances, but our true identity is who God says we are. Documenting our dreams is another form of one-on-one training with God, creating an unbreakable firewall that eliminates the virus of counterfeit communication.

19

Many people come to church for healing, deliverance, and a way to break through existing cycles in their lives. What would the church be like if we used our spiritual gifts to actually serve those who need healing? Instead of providing them a substitute like a class or a Bible study, what if we walked them through how to unlock their freedom forever? Some people are so unhealthy spiritually that it's too risky to place them with a community of other believers because hurt people will hurt people.

Thankfully, the church is a training center to heal the sick, raise the spiritually dead, and cast out demons. Deliverance and healing is the scriptural beginning of the healing process. Counseling, teaching, therapy, yoga, crystals, sage, and medication are not substitutes for deliverance. It's time for believers to stop editing the Bible to hug our fears, euthanize our pet demons, and start editing our lives.

I grew up in a small neighborhood church that primarily preached the good news found in the Gospels. This is the most popular way to understand the heart of the man we know as Jesus Christ, but with good news, there is bad news. Thankfully, the good news is sealed by the victory of Jesus Christ, but that does not eliminate daily opposition and war against the enemy's attacks. It wasn't until much later that I realized the Gospels were just a small fraction of this fascinating book; the rest of the Bible is filled with strategies to activate the gifts of the Holy Spirit. Daniel chapter 10 gives us a glimpse at what a battle looks like in the spiritual realm, and we find out in Ephesians that "a prince of the power of the air" exists. The Bible confirms that unseen aerial warfare exists and that our spiritual gifts are the keys that unlock the weapons we need to shut it down.

Signing up for any kind of battle requires discipline and training. Most battles in the Bible were won by prayer and fasting. Prayer unlocks power, and if we are prayerless, then we are powerless. We need an open line to God, and our prayer is the Wi-Fi between God and us. Prayer to a believer is how we access the Power of God. It's like our oxygen, and we can't live without it. Throughout the Bible, we discover that the biggest battles were conquered by disciplined fasting. These people cleared their systems to eliminate brain fog and hear direct strategy from the Lord. Fasting brings the presence of God closer to us. We can reference how prayer and fasting defeat the enemy in 2 Chronicles Chapter 20 verse 1-23.

Spiritual warfare is the actual battle that silently goes on behind the scenes. Unlike most battles, spiritual warfare is not person-to-person combat but communication between one spirit and another. Unlike most battles, we never see who our opponent is, but we can feel the force of its influence, and the battle is daily. We must train our souls to be masters at the art of this form of battle. The biggest difference between natural warfare and supernatural warfare is that we are on the winning side; it's up to us to show up with an understanding of who our opponent is. The battle is never actually against the person but, instead, the spirit working within them and even within us.

The hardest spiritual warfare battle is the one we have with ourselves on a daily basis. We are constantly battling whether we will choose the high road vs. the "clapback," whether we will drink the green juice vs. the milkshake, and whether we will be obedient and glorify God with our decisions or serve ourselves. This world is full of influences and temptations that cause us to have exhausting battles within our own minds against sin. To effectively win our battles, we must be proficient in the weapons of warfare.

The Full Armor of God

"Finally, be strengthened by the Lord and by his vast strength. Put on the full armor of God so that you can stand against the schemes of the devil. For our struggle is not against flesh and blood, but against the rulers, against the authorities, against the cosmic powers of this darkness, against evil, spiritual forces in the heavens. For this reason take up the full armor of

God, so that you may be able to resist in the evil day, and hav-ing prepared everything, to take your stand. Stand, therefore, with truth like a belt around your waist, righteousness like ar-mor on your chest, and your feet sandaled with readiness for the gospel of peace. In every situation take up the shield of faith with which you can extinguish all the flaming arrows of the evil one. Take the helmet of salvation and the sword of the Spirit—which is the Word of God. Pray at all times in the Spirit with every prayer and request, and stay alert with all persever-ance and intercession for all the saints."

~ *Ephesians 6:10-18 CSB*

The helmet of salvation is one of the first pieces of armor we are advised to put on. The helmet of salvation helps us guard our thoughts and keeps thoughts that are not from God out of our heads. The belt of truth is the piece that holds the armor together. The truth of God's faithfulness makes us stronger be-lievers. It is the truth that sets us free. It is the truth that has the power of deliverance. The breastplate of righteousness protects us from the accusations of the enemy. Our shield of faith comes in handy during difficult conversations. It's the shield of faith that protects us from the painful words (fiery darts) that come from others. Our shoes of readiness give us the ability to walk through difficult situations, and finally, the sword of the spirit is our only offensive weapon. This sword is useless without know-ing the Bible.

Spiritual Downloads (Spiritual Gifts)

Spiritual gifts are from the Holy Spirit and are exclusively given to the church. It's time for believers to unlock their access to the hidden technology God has given us. We must understand that we only have one enemy, Satan. When we unlock the power of our spiritual gifts, we have the key that destroys the enemy's work. We learn in God's Word that there are nine manifestation gifts (1 Corinthians 12:7); these gifts are the most sensational-ized gifts in the world. As believers, we must maintain the pos-ture of using them freely to serve one another since they were freely given to us. People love the manifestation gifts because they demonstrate that the power of God is alive and working.

Then there are six serving gifts (Romans 12:6-8) and five ministry gifts (Ephesians 4:11-13). We also learn that there are nine fruit of the spirit that show up as key evidence that the Holy Spirit is working in our lives. We navigate more toward the gifts we love the most, but we must strengthen the muscle of the gifts that need to be exercised more. Are you equally strong at grant-ing grace to others who have offended you? Is it natural for you to jump in and help someone who stayed behind at a gathering to clean up? There are different kinds of gifts, but the same God distributes them all. We can find references for these gifts all throughout the Bible.

Ministry Gifts	Manifestation Gifts	Serving Gifts
Ephesians 4:11-13	1 Corinthians 12:7	Romans 12:6-8
1 Corinthians 12:28	**The Revelation Gifts**	• Administration
• Apostles	(Reveals information)	• Hospitality
• Evangelist	• Discerning of Spirits	• Mercy
• Prophets	• Word of Wisdom	• Helps
• Pastors	• Word of Knowledge	• Giving
• Teacher	**Inspiration Gifts**	• Service
	(Inspires communication)	
	• Prophecy	
	• Gift of Tongues	
	• Interpretation of Tongues	
	Power Gifts	
	(Performs miracles)	
	• Faith	
	• Healing	
	• Miracles	

"The Holy Spirit is given to each of us in a special way. That is for the good of all. To some people the Spirit gives a message of wisdom. To others the same Spirit gives a message of knowledge. To others the same Spirit gives faith. To others that one Spirit gives gifts of healing. To others he gives the power to do miracles. To others he gives the ability to prophesy. To others he gives the ability to tell the spirits apart. To others he gives the ability to speak in different kinds of languages they had not known before. And to still others he gives the ability to explain what was said in those languages. All the gifts are produced by one and the same Spirit. He gives gifts to each person, just as he decides."

~1 Corinthians 12:7-11 NIRV

Knowing how to operate in every area of these gifts is valuable to our Christian well-being. You probably have already been using these gifts in your everyday life and always thought it was a coincidence, but as Christians, we know better! We know that God loves talking to us, and this is one of the many ways the Holy Spirit unlocks our joy and releases strategy and understanding. You were probably most active with your gifts as a child. God loves to use child-like imagination.

Did you love to play doctor and heal your stuffed animals? Were you the teacher of your imaginary class? Did you paint and draw beautiful visuals that brought you joy as you created them? Maybe you were the child who always "spoke very wise for your age?" Or you could have been that child who always knew something was going to happen before it actually did because God showed you in your dreams. Here's a brief overview of how each gift works.

Revelation Gifts

Words of Wisdom is when you receive a supernatural understanding that leads to your success and the success of others. Words of wisdom are the key to unlocking a creative strategy for solving problems and references the present as well as events of the future. This gift is not only useful for yourself; it's a gift that most counselors, advisers, life coaches, and people in leadership naturally have and share with others to develop life-enhancing strategies.

Words of Knowledge is very similar to Words of Wisdom, but the biggest difference is that you usually have no prior information regarding a person, place, or thing. Suddenly, you can share knowledge about something that is usually hidden during the conversation. Words of Knowledge reflects on the present and the past. Someone might mention that their arm is hurting, and God immediately shows you which arm is in pain. You can confirm it or just begin to pray for that specific area.

Another example is as you pray for someone, God may show you a picture of something like a car or a house. With this information, you can confirm with the person what you are seeing. If they can confirm that it relates to their life, you can pray with them even more specifically about it. This gift is sometimes associated with a visual, a smell, a touch, or a feeling. The gift of Words of Wisdom and Words of Knowledge should not be confused with the gift of prophecy.

Let's talk about the gift of Discerning of Spirits. It's the last revelation gift in this group and is also referred to as distinguishing between spirits. Discerning of spirits is not the same as discernment. Discernment is a part of our natural instinct to sense when something is not right. Discerning of spirits is a revelation gift that is highly sensitive when you are in the company of others. This gift is the key to clearly see the difference in an influence from God, Satan, the world, and ourselves. Romans 12:2

says that people with this gift renew their minds often by testing things to determine the will of God, what is good and acceptable and perfect. This gift should not be used against others as a tool of personal judgment but should empower Christians to immediately intercede against the spirit that has been identified in someone else.

The Bible never speaks about "vibes" or "vibrations" in the atmosphere; however, it's very clear about the spirit of good and evil. People with this gift can identify areas of oppression within other Christians. Knowing this allows them access to specific areas for intercessory prayers toward victory instead of defeat in someone's life. This gift is also a key to sensing when an angel or the Holy Spirit himself has entered the atmosphere.

Inspiration Gifts

The spiritual gift of Prophecy can be expressed by the entire church. The Bible states that it is the greatest gift of them all. I believe this is because this gift is used to build up the church with three specific goals— to edify, build up, and provide comfort. The gift of prophecy is distributed to anyone who believes by the will of God. We can confirm this in 1 Corinthians 14:30-31.

The gift of Exhortation is one of my personal favorites because it's a gift of joy. People with this gift are always living in expectation of "the good stuff" because they firmly believe that our victory is in how the story ends. They can naturally bring people closer to God. People with the gift of exhortation come off as positive because they are naturally wired to encourage and strengthen themselves and others. They always highlight Jesus' amazing work and promises so we don't have to worry about the small stuff. This gift also reminds believers that the God we serve is the only one who transforms and renews our hearts and minds. People with this gift are highly resourceful and can be counted on for all the "how to" and "where can I find" types of questions.

The gift of Tongues and the gift of Interpreting Tongues are both pretty amazing to see in action. The gift of diverse tongues is for the languages here on earth. Someone can be gifted in learning multiple languages to communicate with others quickly. These people can often instantly speak a foreign language they have never spoken before. Another gift of tongues is when we unlock our God-given heavenly language to speak to God. This is a personal communication between God and us. Next is the gift of tongues spoken in a corporate setting. This usually happens when God uses one person to give the church a message and another person to interpret the message. The person corporately speaking in tongues should not interpret their own message because there is no evidence that they are communicating with God without an interpreter.

The Power Gifts

The gift of Faith is used to encourage, empower, or motivate someone. Faith is given to every believer by the saving grace of God, but the gift of Faith is a special endowment of confidence in God's promises. It's an unshakable faith in the written Word of God. These people are fearlessly humble, outgoing, and love to connect with others to offer encouragement. Examples of this person would be a coach, a pastor, a teacher, or someone in military leadership. We serve a God who creates and establishes leaders!

The gift of Miracles that took place when Jesus Christ walked the earth might look a little different nowadays. A miracle is an event that occurs outside of natural boundaries. People who operate in this gift have rare and incredible life stories that make you realize that you ain't seen nothing yet! You might not see water being turned into wine or loaves of bread and fish being multiplied; however, that same faith still produces miraculous outcomes. A person operating in the gift of miracles usually sees extraordinary things happen through them to solve problems either for themselves or others.

Such people are humble in their character, will always point others to Jesus Christ and never take the credit or glory. I experienced the gift of healing in a meeting with a few women. One of the women said she was having severe back pain and wanted us to pray for her. My arms were sore from working out the day prior. A different woman stood up and walked over to the lady with severe back pain and began praying for her. As she prayed, you could feel the atmosphere shift. When she finished, not only was the woman's back pain gone, but my soreness disappeared too! The whole room began to talk about how minor pains they had at the beginning of the meeting were gone. God might also give someone knowledge of how to use the earth's elements to develop a lasting cure for illnesses and diseases. The gifts of healing and miracles can be seen in action through our physicians, chemists, pharmacists, and even our military.

Service Gifts

"But earnestly desire and strive for the greater gifts [if acquiring them is going to be your goal]. And yet I will show you a still more excellent way [one of the choicest graces and the highest of them all: unselfish love]."
~ *1 Corinthians 12:31 AMP*

Christians are called to live lives that are "decent and in order" in 1 Corinthians 14:40. To show us exactly what this looks like, God has given people the gifted passion to keep their lives and the lives of others in order with the gift of Administration. This is a gift of leadership, and people with this gift are very strong in executing a vision. Organizing, strategizing, and management in teams, groups, or for themselves just comes naturally. People with this gift must be intentionally mindful that they do not fall into a competitive and controlling mindset; this gift is a serving gift.

Very similar to the gift of Administration is the gift of Hospitality. This gift is usually seen in people who have a natural desire to plan a celebration. They find a reason to celebrate anything and everything—from a newborn baby down to a new pair of shoes! The gift of hospitality allows someone to instantly love a stranger and open up their homes to family and friends. They love to feed others and also take the time to sit and fellowship with you; they love making others feel welcome and comfortable. This gift can be used to serve others outside of the home.

The gift of Mercy is a special ability to feel compassion and empathy not only for believers but the entire human race. People with a gift of mercy cheerfully work at being a reflection of the love of Jesus Christ. It's nothing for them to hop in the car and go visit or offer up their assistance to a new mommy, an elderly person, or someone grieving or in pain. They serve others from a place of genuine love.

People with the service gift of Helps are passionate about being plugged into the needs of the church wherever and whenever they can. They prefer to serve behind the scenes to help those with ministry gifts remain focused on the main task of the ministry.

As believers, we all give tithes and offerings; however, people with the gift of Giving naturally have joy and delight in going above and beyond the ten percent. They find ways to increase and scatter their income as needed, with the understanding in Deuteronomy 8:18 that "God gives us the ability to create wealth" and abundance. Since it's God's money, they are excellent stewards with God's financial increase. These people share what they have with faith, knowing that God will replenish their needs and greatly increase them.

Lastly, let's discuss the fruit of the Spirit. *"But the fruit of the Spirit is love, joy, peace, patience, kindness, goodness, faithfulness, gentleness, self-control; against such things there is no law." ~ Galatians ESV 5:22-23*

We find evidence of whether we are using our spiritual gifts correctly based on the fruit that our spirit naturally produces. This evidence confirms that we are operating in alignment with the Holy Spirit in our gifting and is known as the "Fruit of the Spirit." Think of a tree as the Spiritual gift of the Holy Spirit and the fruit of the spirit as the physical character trait that comes out of the tree.

Ministry Gifts

"And he gave the apostles, the prophets, the evangelists, the shepherds and teachers, to equip the saints for the work of ministry, for building up the body of Christ, until we all attain to the unity of the faith and of the knowledge of the Son of God, to mature manhood, to the measure of the stature of the fullness of Christ,"
~Ephesians 4:11-13 ESV

The Apostle Paul writes this as if he knows that, over time, the church will become unraveled and scattered. The church will need people to diligently seek training and understanding. Paul mentions in Ephesians 4 that some people have a special gifting to equip the saints. This gifting is known as ministry gifts—Prophet, Teacher, Evangelist, Apostle, and Pastor.

People who serve the church with ministry gifts are God's gift to the church. They help the church discover and execute their gifts and operate based on function and purpose and not by a title. God designed these people in the womb and set them apart to bring revelation, empower believers, and build his kingdom here on earth. People with ministry gifts have a natural wiring to build the kingdom with joy. Every church should have these people available for regular developmental conversations. People with ministry gifts are a key component in understanding our walk with Christ.

A prophet has been called by God to the ministry office of the church. Prophets know a prophet when they see one. This same spiritual connection holds true for the rest of those called into what is known as the "five-fold ministry, which includes the teacher, the apostle, the pastor, and the evangelist. In Deuteronomy 18:15-22, we learn that when a prophet delivers a message in the name of the Lord, it should be accurate, or the consequence is death. God does not play when it comes to falsely communicating his Word. This is why the prophet or the gift of prophecy should not be confused with a psychic, fortuneteller, or tarot card reader. We can confirm in scripture that the Trinity (Father, Son, Holy Spirit) is not the source of knowledge for anyone involved in occult practices or practices that cannot be backed up with scripture.

We can learn a lot about apostles and the gift of apostleship from the Apostle Paul, Peter, James, John, Ananias, Phillip, Barnabas, and Matthew. By definition, the Apostle is one who actually witnessed the ministry of Jesus Christ and his resurrection. The gift of apostleship continues in the same way.

The mission for those with the gift of apostleship today is to create new ministries and churches, go into areas where the gospel is not preached, reach across cultures to establish churches in challenging environments, raise up and develop leaders, and call out and lead pastors. These are leaders of leaders and ministers of ministers. They are influencers; they are entrepreneurial and can take risks and perform difficult tasks.

Teachers have a unique way of sharing the gospel, enabling them to make the Bible text relatable to life situations. Teachers are sensitive to not add words to or remove words from Scripture. They find joy in sharing the entire text. Teachers believe that the Bible is far better than Netflix and Hulu because it is true history and mystery full of action, passion, romance, and drama. Natural-born teachers can spot false claims of the Bible and correct the error before it turns a new believer away from the church.

Evangelism is a gift. As I began studying the Bible, I grew a strong desire to share the gospel, but only with people who believed that Jesus Christ is the Son of God. That isn't quite what evangelism is. The ministry gift of Evangelism allows people to communicate with all types of people without reservation. Evangelists can easily memorize Scripture to engage in conversations of truth with others. They have a heart to connect with non-believers in engaging conversations about Jesus Christ. Evangelists fearlessly look for relationships with those who don't know Jesus and are open to the leading of the Holy Spirit to approach different people. It brings them joy to share the goodness of God with others.

The Pastor or Shepherd is the last ministry gift on the list. People with this gift assume the lifelong responsibility for the spiritual welfare of a group of believers. Pastors watch over, guide, train, and nurture other believers in their spiritual growth and in the work of the ministry. I remember hesitating to join fairly large churches because I believed I needed to have a personal relationship with the person holding the microphone. After conquering my fears and being obedient about planting my feet at a church, I learned that the pastor equipped several other pastors to meet with every member of the church regardless of the need.

If I hadn't trusted where God was leading me, I would have never conquered the fear of being connected to a megachurch. Did you know that the first megachurch was developed in the Book of Acts? The disciples of Jesus Christ began sharing the gospel, and their audience began multiplying by the thousands. It is in God's nature to add to the church, subtract from the church, and multiply the church. This is called GOD Math. He does not create division in the church. Where there is division, the enemy is somewhere in the mix.

Documenting Our Dreams

"For God speaks again and again though people do not recognize it. He speaks in dreams, in visions of the night, when deep sleep falls on people as they lie in their beds."

~ *Job 33: 14-15 NLT*

Nothing is as it seems. In our dreams, God provides one-on-one strategies that equip us for things to come. The Bible documents the history of God, but through our relationship with God, our dreams reveal the mysteries of God—mysteries about our lives, mysteries about the company we keep, and mysteries about the times and seasons. Not only does God reveal the keys that unlock a strategy, but he also gives us a visual outline to follow to navigate our battles.

God also selects the weapon for us to use. Do you see why documenting our dreams is imperative to our daily function as believers? Our dreams are messages from God, and one message can change our entire life. God always speaks to us in dreams and visions. Our dreams wake up our eyes and open our ears to what he is trying to communicate to us. Our dreams also provide warnings for upcoming challenges that God wants to give specific instructions for. We don't want to miss our moment for alignment with God. "Random dreams" usually have a hidden message, so we must take all of the randoms before God.

The Book of Daniel is a good reference for studying how our dreams are one-on-one strategies with God. Dreams are a form of kingdom technology that God gives us to unlock the strategy he gives us in our dreams. As Daniel grows up, he begins to have so much wisdom and prophetic dreams. He made the unpopular choice to fast and pray for a clear strategy and practice extreme faith. I use the phrase extreme faith because Daniels's life was on the line several times. This extreme faith was connected to many miracles.

Write it and make it plain—every detail in our dreams matters. The dog, the pumpkin, the year and make of the car, the number of items, the color of the door and the sky—all of it matters. It's also important to remember and document our emotions while we dream. Did we feel sadness, were we afraid, did we have peace? Our dreams are the beginning. Once we document our dreams, we have decided to enter into the conversation with God. The vision becomes clearer.

My family uses the book *The Divinity Code,* written by Adam Thompson and Adrian Beale, to help us identify the message in our dreams. This book is written by followers of Jesus Christ, Adam F. Thompson and Adrian Beale. I specify this because books are often written about dreams and visions by people who have committed their lives to the occult and receive demonic strategy. Believers are warned throughout the Bible not to mix occultic practices with Christianity.

Setting the atmosphere for dreams before going to bed is a key to producing the most vivid dreams for me. One way to set the atmosphere for dreams is to put your spirit in a posture to hear a message from the Lord. Create and commit to setting an atmosphere to hear from God. If bedtime is normally around 9 p.m., your schedule might begin around 7 or 8 p.m. This must be a very intentional routine because God always has something to say to us and about us.

My routine is to close all my apps and alerts and turn on a playlist of my favorite worship songs one hour before bedtime. On another night, setting the atmosphere might be playing an audio Bible before falling asleep. Next, I have a method for documenting my dreams. I recommend either using a note-taking app on your phone or writing on a notepad what you are visualizing and hearing.

It might be a little difficult at first to wake up to record our dreams because our dreams usually come in our deepest times of sleep. Waking ourselves up to document our dreams is a muscle that requires ongoing training until we get better and better at doing so. Not wanting to wake up ourselves to record strategy from God is a form of warfare against us, so we must be intentional about documenting everything. God wants us to know him on a personal level. He has a hilarious sense of humor that he wants us to become familiar with.

The Word of God Is the Firewall

Before we get too deep into the topic of spiritualism, I must be very clear and intentional when sharing information about spirituality. It's important to note that I am specifically talking about the acts of the Holy Spirit. The Father, the Son of God Jesus Christ, and the Holy Spirit. We know this as the Trinity. If we are followers of Jesus Christ and have chosen Christianity, we have chosen to follow the instructions in the Bible. The Bible is very clear about how serious God is about his relationship with us.

To say God is a jealous God is just one way of explaining it, but I would like to create a few more common everyday examples for you. You know how it feels to spend quality time with a loved one and then someone abruptly interrupts your visit? Here's another—it's that feeling that you get when your closest friend develops a new relationship with someone else, and you wonder if this new friend has the best intentions for your friend. Will they be able to keep them safe?

The idea of us in relationships with other gods and spirits is similar to the level of jealousy you would feel if you found out that your spouse was having an affair. Finally, imagine your child calling a total stranger Mom or Dad. No matter how people try to remix the fact that the God we serve does not allow other gods, we must be wise enough to always remember that God's Word is truth. Here's one passage in Deuteronomy 18 that lets us know how he feels about sharing his children with other gods and spirits.

"When you come into the land that the Lord your God is giving you, you shall not learn to follow the abominable practices of those nations. There shall not be found among you anyone who burns his son or his daughter as an offering, anyone who practices divination or tells fortunes or interprets omens, or a sorcerer or a charmer or a medium or a necromancer or one who inquires of the dead, for whoever does these things is an abomination to the Lord. And because of these abominations the Lord your God is driving them out before you. You shall be blameless before the Lord your God, for these nations, which you are about to dispossess, listen to fortune-tellers and to diviners. But as for you, the Lord your God has not allowed you to do this."

~ Deuteronomy 18:9-14 ESV

Abomination - extreme disgust. ~ Merriam Webster Dictionary

Since God is the creator of all things, it would be wise to get our power from the source itself instead of using "spiritually charged tools" that can be purchased from a spiritual bookstore or herbal store. Since God is the creator, it would be wise to admire the creator instead of worshipping the things that the creator creates. An example of a "spiritually charged tool" could be a crystal, book, or a deck of cards purchased from a new age store vs. finding it in its natural habitat outside on the ground. Even then, its previous ownership is questionable.

In my lifetime, I have seen people seek power from the tiniest things that God has created, like rocks, crystals, and even dirt in a jar. Historically, Satan has been known to create the counterfeit version of everything discussed in the Bible. He even has his own form of the Bible. Since we know that a knock-off of Christianity exists, we must be aware of it all the time. Since our God has adopted us as his children, he has given us access to everything we need to conquer our everyday obstacles and challenges.

The Power that God directly gives us is greater than any prayer over a stone or plant. God created every sparkle in that rock, so we must praise the creator for creating the beauty of elements like fire, earth, water, and wind. Unfortunately, we are born with sin into a sinful world, and we unknowingly begin life backward. We are trained at very young ages to connect with the natural world first instead of including God as the super part of our natural experience. As children, we are fascinated with counterfeit superheroes before we even get the opportunity to learn who the real superhero is. How different would childhood be if we learned about Samson and all his mighty strength before we learned about Satan's counterfeit mutant creation, the Incredible Hulk?

We grow up training our minds to chase the ambitions of our hearts' desires instead of chasing the heart of God. God created us to be world changers and dream builders, but we get buried, booked, and busy with digesting what the world is feeding us while only sipping on God's Word here and there. This should work the other way around. We get locked into these unnecessary organizations and relationships to gain leverage in a society that will chew us up and spit us out with no remorse. We lack the knowledge that a relationship with God is the only leverage we need because we are either not exercising our authority or unaware that it exists. God is the one who appoints us. God is the one who positions us. God gives us authority, dominion, and power over all living things. It's God.

Our relationship with the one true living God should be the main course; his Word is the main source of nourishment on our plates. This is how some people can fast for weeks on liquids, prayer, and Scripture because they are full of God's spirit. I love how it's written in the Bible, as if he is letting us in on a secret that he has given us the biggest advantage over our opponent. Check it out:

"Look, I have given you authority over all the power of the enemy, and you can walk among snakes and scorpions and crush them. Nothing will injure you."

~ *Luke 10:19 NLT*

Eliminating the Virus

"Finally, be strong in the Lord and in the strength of his might. Put on the whole armor of God, that you may be able to stand against the schemes of the devil. For we do not wrestle against flesh and blood, but against the rulers, against the authorities, against the cosmic powers over this present darkness, against the spiritual forces of evil in the heavenly places."

~ *Ephesians 6:10-12 ESV*

I love how the Apostle Paul begins this verse with "Finally."

I can't bring this chapter to a close without letting you know about possible items in your home that create a bridge into your life from evil dimensions. These items are earthbound, and demons have the legal authority to attach themselves to these objects. These items contain spiritual properties that contain an influence that will create chaos in our lives.

Below, you will see a list of Satan's counterfeit "spiritual gifts" and objects that can position you out of alignment with God and in alignment with the other gods, which the Bible warns us about. If you have any of these items in your home, it is likely the reason you feel a lack of peace, brain fog, heaviness in the atmosphere, an addictive pull to sin, anxiety, depression or an unsound mind, poor spiritual discernment, or feeling disconnected to God. You can continue reading about this in both Leviticus 19:26-31 and Deuteronomy 18:9-14. These items should not be resold because the influence connected to them spreads like a slow virus that attacks our spirit and eventually shuts down and disables our ability to hear clearly from God. Burn these items immediately.

Any Hindu objects, shiva idols, false gods, idols, and statues of Buddha

- Hindu sculptures
- Dragons
- Fairies
- Elves
- Gnomes (including those sitting outside the home)
- Mermaids (a.k.a. Marine Spirits)
- Pagan gods

- Greek Mythology gods
- Crystals
- Balls
- Wands
- Jewelry
- Stones
- Any crystal used for divination and witchcraft

If you have any books with the following topics, I advise you to burn them immediately

- The Occult
- Kemetic Mysticism
- Spell casting
- Magic or magick
- New Age
- Astrology
- Esoteric books
- Gnostic
- Transcendentalism
- Yoga books

- Books about crystals
- Aliens
- Universalism
- Pantheism
- Drugs
- Spiritualism
- Sorcery
- Channeling
- Spiritual awakening
- Atlantis

Fiction/children's books that contain any of the above.

Music

- Meditation music that includes chanting.
- Mood altering music that influences feelings of sadness, depression, and anger

Clothing
- Graphic images of symbols
- Graphic images of false gods

Miscellaneous home items
- Tapestry
- Posters
- Jewelry
- Dream catchers (we don't want anything catching our dreams)
- Sage burning
- Pendants

Here's what God's Word has to say concerning these things.

"For the desires of the flesh are against the Spirit, and the desires of the Spirit are against the flesh, for these are opposed to each other, to keep you from doing the things you want to do. But if you are led by the Spirit, you are not under the law. Now the works of the flesh are evident: sexual immorality, impurity, sensuality, idolatry, sorcery, enmity, strife, jealousy, fits of anger, rivalries, dissensions, divisions, envy, drunkenness, orgies, and things like these. I warn you, as I warned you before, that those who do such things will not inherit the kingdom of God. But the fruit of the Spirit is love, joy, peace, patience, kindness, goodness, faithfulness, gentleness, self-control; against such things there is no law."

~ Galatians 5:17-23 ESV

Take a look at this one too:

"And he said to me, "It is done! I am the Alpha and the Omega, the beginning and the end. To the thirsty I will give from the spring of the water of life without payment. The one who conquers will have this heritage, and I will

be his God and he will be my son. But as for the cowardly, the faithless, the detestable, as for murderers, the sexually immoral, sorcerers, idolaters, and all liars, their portion will be in the lake that burns with fire and sulphur, which is the second death."

> ~ *Revelation 21:6-8 ESV*

A second death? No, thank you! These items also need to be burned if they are in your home or the homes of loved ones

- Ouija Boards
- Playing cards
- Tarot cards
- Angel, fairy, elf card decks
- Oracle decks
- Master decks
- Ascended master decks
- Fortune-telling decks
- Magic card decks

I know you are probably thinking, not my Spades cards! and *Not Uno*! Think about the emotion fueled when playing card games. Would you be more reserved if God was sitting at the table playing cards with you? Another thing to consider regarding card decks is the origin of the game.

2 Corinthians 4:4 = In their case the god of this world has blinded the minds of the unbelievers, to keep them from seeing the light of the gospel of the glory of Christ, who is the image of God.

Whatever gift God has naturally given you—music, art, singing, writing, fashion, fitness, etc., use it to destroy hell. Remain teachable and be open to the fact that this walk is an evolving walk of faith. God will use your skills. Obey him in the face of criticism. Remember that your friends didn't call you to serve the kingdom. God called you.

Let's Pray:

Father God, you are the miraculous creator of all things in heaven and on earth. Lord, there are parts of me that do not want to understand the spiritual realm because it seems too scary and dark. However, I do realize that I am not where you want me to be. I want to understand what it takes to be victorious in all battles that are seen and unseen. So I ask, Lord Jesus, give me a discerning spirit that equips me to become victorious. Open my eyes to see and my ears to hear all of the one-on-one strategies you give to me. Keep my heart and mind focused on the will of God. Protect me from the tricks and schemes of darkness. Lord, reveal to me the mysteries that you want me to know tonight in my dreams. May all understanding come from reading and knowing your living Word in the Bible. Thank you for winning all of my battles that are seen and unseen.

In Jesus' name, amen.

"So God created man in his own image, in the image of God he created him; male and female he created them."
~ *Genesis 1:27 ESV*

Chapter Four

IDENTITY

What Is Modesty Anyway?

In my younger years, image and identity were important to me. I wanted to connect with the woman that God designed. A major part of my identity was my relationships with my family and friends. It might not seem like it, but the people we surround ourselves with have a huge influence on how we view ourselves and almost everything else.

At an early age, I noticed my body required daily activity to stay strong physically and mentally. I was on the flag squad in the marching band, and my friends and me jokingly stress out about our bodies back then, wishing we had those same bodies today. Our marching band director always hinted in a fatherly way when we were picking up the desserts a little too much. In return, we would hit the track during the week to fix that.

I needed to do sit-ups to maintain my waistline, so every night before bed, I placed my feet underneath an opening in my dresser to create pressure on my feet. I always did two sets of thirty sit-ups. I managed to accomplish my high school years with a flat stomach, but one thing that never has been flat is my butt. The women on my father's side of the family are all blessed with shapely bodies. At an early age, all of us were blessed with the bang and the boom of the full figure.

I don't think that my mother was ready for the bottom half of the body that God gave me, so not only were sit-ups a part of my nightly routine, but I also had to do something called sit-walks. Sit walks is a movement that requires you to sit on the floor and walk on your butt cheeks from one wall in the room to the other wall in the room. I did four laps each night. People thought this workout was a butt deflator, but it actually had the opposite effect. Sit-walks and *Buns of Steel* actually increased the size of my butt and made me insecure about attending church. Both men and women would turn their heads and watch my body as I navigated my way through the sanctuary.

As a young Christian woman, my body insecurity used to make me very uncomfortable around other Christians. I was taught by other Christians to "cover up" so I would not "offend" the church, but wasn't my body God's body too? It was most imperative that I did not "tempt" male leaders of the church with my body. In my case, that meant merely attending church would cause men to be tempted to sin. The deception behind that burns me up now as I share it with you because that type of thinking has nothing to do with God.

When I attended church fully covered from head to toe, male and female ushers would evaluate me and seat me toward the back of the church. I eventually got fed up with that kind of judgment and insisted on a better view. I spent years investing in clothes that were "not offensive" to others in the church, only to remain offensive to others in the church. I began idolizing how I appeared instead of learning about how God truly saw me.

I was more accepted by people who did not attend church more than those who claimed to be followers of Jesus Christ. Anyone with a similar experience should leave this kind of church immediately. All souls matter, and no one should be discouraged about building a relationship with God. These types of churches clearly have not discovered the truth of the gospel and falsely teach about fleshly identity vs. our identity in Christ. Transformation begins with the soul. I did not wear any jeans or shorts for over six years of my adult life because of this thought process of "protecting men from sin and lust," which I later learned had nothing to do with me. A woman cannot make a man unwillingly sin. To even make this thought make sense, we would have to believe that men aren't independent thinkers. God describes man as his masterpiece, not some soulless body that is tossed around in lust and confusion. It is up to us to intentionally master characteristics like self-control, patience, and kindness so that we can walk out our faith, deliverance, and lust no more.

During this time, I made sure I purchased ankle-length A-line skirts. Dresses and skirts were always below my knees, and tops were blouses that did not draw attention to my upper torso. I was still labeled a "sexy Christian" in my twenties. A sexy Christian who was actually abstaining from sex!

I finally had enough of this cycle of selecting clothes that did not "offend others" and started wearing clothes that matched the inner joy I had about myself and made me look beautiful. As I started learning how to use my Bible as a teaching tool, I began to have a problem with this theory of "offending the body of Christ with the body God gave me." This teaching is nowhere in the Bible and is a complete lie. After fifteen years of listening to the biblical understanding and teachings from others, I decided to get some understanding of my own from the Word of God.

Once I cracked open my own Bible and began studying the truth for myself, I started by learning about the word "modesty" heavily used in religious communities. A common definition of modesty is a behavior, manner, or appearance intended to avoid impropriety or indecency. Surely I was not intentionally leaving the house with the goal of being inappropriate or indecent, especially since church was my destination. Next, I looked at what God's Word says about modesty.

First, let's look at the most popular scripture used for modesty today, 1 Timothy 2:9-10. This scripture is spoken by one of the most famous apostles in the Bible, the Apostle Paul. Now, if anyone could educate us about transformation, the proof is in the pudding with him. The following scripture has instructions for both men and women.

"I desire then that in every place the men should pray, lifting holy hands without anger or quarreling; likewise also that women should adorn themselves in respectable apparel, with modesty and self-control, not with braided hair and gold or pearls or costly attire, but with what is proper for women who profess godliness—with good works."
~ 1 Timothy 2:8-10 ESV

Let's unpack the information here in reference to the woman. Paul is speaking of the posture of both women and men. This was also during a time when women were intentionally drawing attention to themselves with elaborate, eye-catching hairstyles that took the focus of worship and Bible study from the teacher and on to them. The most important thing about this scripture is that these women were trying to arouse the men or even catch the eye of a covetous woman with their "pearls and costly attire." Today, the equivalent of 1 Timothy 2:9-10 would be if a woman showed up to church in a two-piece bikini and walked down to the front of the church to hear the sermon. No. Paul was not having any of that!

Using 1 Timothy 2:9-10 as a weapon against a woman based on personal insecurity or sinful nature is wrong. In other countries with different dress standards, women can be fully covered and still be victims of sexual harassment and abuse. As I matured biblically and culturally, I realized that the issue of modesty was not a dress code issue but a sin issue. It was a character issue. Essentially, I was protecting those who needed to get their spirit of lust, rape, and abuse in check. No more of that. You can wear respectable apparel and be inappropriate and indecent in your behavior. This is what Paul was talking about in 1 Timothy 2:9-10.

Confidently Fearless

"Charm is deceitful, and beauty is vain but a woman who fears the Lord is to be praised."
                                   ~ Proverbs 31:30 ESV

Ladies, listen, any man who is aware of the truths of the Bible will praise a woman that fully submits to Jesus Christ. When we understand our identity, we are irresistible to believers and non-believers. The fruit of the Holy Spirit is the gift that God gives us. The right one will appreciate your character of righteousness and your desire to cast all of your concerns toward God instead of him... because what can he do?

Modesty is not about physical attraction and beauty. It is about decreasing the desire to "Walk the Runway" when entering the sanctuary and more about posturing ourselves to receive everything the Holy Spirit releases while we are in the building. Modesty is about having dignity and honor toward our bodies. It's also about respecting your future husband and positioning him to fall in love with you unconditionally and for the right reasons.

We are in the time of the internet, mobile phones, and screenshots. History has a tendency to resurface with a vengeance. Modesty is about staying within your budget and stewarding the wealth God has given you. Let the Joneses do their own thing, and don't try to keep up. Purchasing the same $1,000 shoes that the pastor's wife wore is not being authentic to the woman God specifically designed you to be. It's idolatry and coveting, and you don't want those kinds of problems. Encountering God can be an overwhelming experience sometimes. Some of us kick our shoes off to run, some of us start dancing like David danced, and some of us get emotional and tears start to smear all of that makeup that took thirty minutes or more to put on.

The young woman had a beautiful figure and was lovely to look at.

~ *Esther 2:7*

Don't get it twisted—our Bible is full of baddies. "Baddies" is a slang term that describes women who are beautiful from head to toe. My identity during my teenage years might have gone a little different if I had learned about Queen Esther from a woman who could make it relatable to the times we were in. The Book of Esther is a great place to start to understand the appearance and attraction of a real woman of the Bible. In Esther, we read that it was a common practice for women to moisturize their skin with perfumed oils. We also learn that women enjoyed applying cosmetics, and the men enjoyed giving them the cosmetics. The beautification process described in Esther was more than just a forty-five-minute to two-hour appointment at the salon. These women were pampered for twelve months at a time. Ladies, let's love on ourselves as often as we can, just like the women in our user's manual, the Bible.

Christian identity theft is a dangerous problem that we have to cancel. This kind of identity theft has nothing to do with your credit but has everything to do with your soul.

Astrology will have you walking around claiming you are a toxic disease called cancer, that you're double-minded like a Gemini, or whatever else is on that list of lies. It's counterfeit to who God says you are. Do you know that we have the authority to determine our day? Better yet, do you know that God will remove every negative trait passed out by astrology when we renew our hearts and our minds? Listen to what is true. The truth comes from the Word of God. We operate differently from the world. We are not the same.

Knowing who God created us to be and how God truly sees us as his creation is the foundation of our "Godfidence," a.k.a. our confidence in who God created us to be. Once we are aware of our biblical identity, no one will be able to convince us otherwise. The world is full of people who want to tell you who you are and what you will become. I challenge you to discover your identity directly from the creator. Here's a snippet of who God says you are:

You are approved (2 Tim. 2:25).	You are called (Gal. 5:13).
You are accepted (Acts 10:35).	You are an overcomer (1 John 5:4).
You are God's friend (John 15:15).	You are free (Luke 4:18).
You are chosen (1 Peter 2:4).	You are an heir to the throne (Rom. 8:17).
You are sealed (Eph. 1:13).	
You are a new creation (2 Cor. 5:17).	You are a disciple of God (John 8:31).
You are adopted by God, which makes you his daughter/son (Eph. 1:5 and Deuteronomy 14:1).	You are blessed (Psalms112:1).
	You are redeemed (Gal. 3:13).

"Don't you realize that your body is the temple of the Holy Spirit, who lives in you and was given to you by God? You do not belong to yourself."
~ *1 Corinthians 6:19*

Design Your Life

Establishing a personal "glam squad" is a great way to be intentional about the maintenance of our bodies. Our glam squad is not only about our outer appearance but about beautifying our souls.

The way we feel on the inside reflects how we feel on the outside, and no one has created any type of cosmetic to cover that up. A great way to start establishing your glam squad is to begin with the inside.

Log on to your computer and search for reviews and information about primary physicians. These are medical professionals who work with their patients to provide regular exams and screenings. They help us manage or often eliminate common health problems, provide prescriptions, and more. Adding a primary physician to the glam squad establishes an ongoing relationship with someone who can provide educational medical feedback when we experience changes in our bodies. Once you have a good list of physicians and reviews to choose from, pray over their names to include God in this decision; after all, it is his body. Ask him which doctor is best for you? He will respond. Our health is our wealth, and we must make sure our bodies are in alignment with God's will for our lives.

Did you know that our oral health affects our entire body? It's a scary thought to imagine someone drilling and scraping our gums and scrubbing our teeth, but the reality is people notice our mouths first. People who share the gospel of Jesus Christ are usually sharing it with large groups of people, and our mouths can't be a distraction from the message. Next on the glam squad is the dentist. Our smile is one of the first things that draws people, and having clean teeth when we speak to others is important. Dental visits usually happen twice a year, and visiting a dentist regularly will not only keep our mouths healthy and our teeth bright, but our whole body. Routine dental care prevents things like tooth decay and gum disease, which is detected by X-rays. Our body houses the Holy Spirit, and the smallest mismanagement will throw us out of alignment.

> *"Physical training is good, but training for godliness is much better, promising benefits in this life and in the life to come."*
>
> ~ *1 Timothy 4:8 NLT*

Finding a health coach was the key that unlocked my increase in daily productivity. I didn't just want a personal trainer but someone who knew the truth about resetting and maintaining God's bodies. After praying for God to send me someone who trained and healed based on God's Word, she showed up on my screen. I was attending an online conference where we had twenty-second meet and greets during the intermission, and she popped on my screen. We connected because we were both writers. Little did I know that she was creating an entire platform about health and lifestyle maintenance.

See what happens when you add God into the situation? We never know how important it is for us to walk with someone through our journey until we're in relationship with God and he begins to hold our hands. God will guide us to the necessities. A health coach takes the time to discover how our bodies respond to nutrition and fitness, and just like Queen Esther, this process can go beyond a six-month fix. A health coach walks with us to kill bad habits, to introduce and maintain every habit that makes our bodies thrive. Our bodies respond beautifully when we give them the fuel they need.

Once we have that part of our glam squad complete, it is time to focus on the outer appearance. I hope you see now how our lives thrive on relationships. The enemy would love for us to isolate ourselves and completely ignore the training that God set before us in the Gospels regarding creating and maintaining relationships.

Isolating ourselves limits the abundance of life God wants us to have, and isolation also causes us to live based on our own understanding. Isolation is Satan's playground. Once we understand how to establish and maintain good relationships, we will begin to see an abundance of people showing up in our lives to help us become who God created us to be. Other key players in our glam squad are ongoing relationships with our beauticians, estheticians, chiropractors, etc. Apply the same practice of praying prior to selection.

Another habit I've been intentional about is visualizing my prayers. I do this by creating prayer boards and prayer lists that I can always look at as the year progresses. Vision boards have gotten so many opposing opinions in the Christian community, but they should not be created to remind God what we need. Instead, they remind us to stay focused on specific aspects of our spiritual walk. God gives us great visions. Laying them out with a pen and paper or actually finding pictures of the visions that God gives us ultimately keeps us and our prayers on track.

A written vision helps us with our accomplishments. If we don't write the vision down, then we can quickly forget about taking it to God in prayer for his strategy. For example, someone with a professional goal to become a doctor might create a board displaying the steps they need to take to achieve the goal. Whatever your title, your board of visual goals will have nothing to do with telling God what you want from him, because he already knows. The board becomes a reminder of our prayers and our progress.

The Bible verse of 1 Timothy 4:8 encourages the training of our spirit. Investing time into our spiritual wellness benefits us so much. We can't pour from an empty place, and if we attempt to encourage others from a place of brokenness, the cracks begin to show. Healing, deliverance, and investing time into our spiritual growth have been game changers for securing peace, joy, and maintaining our happiness. As we get older, we find out that we have to unlearn and uproot all the weeds that have unknowingly been planted in us from our childhood and early adult years.

We must be intentional about uprooting toxic weeds, so we must connect with someone willing to stir up the root of our issues so that the seeds they plant have good soil to grow in. It doesn't matter how often we hop into our cars and head to the sanctuary if we are not open and teachable toward the people God sends to us. Thankfully, believers have been diligently putting their heads and prayers together, and we now have many ways to stay connected. We can fellowship virtually and receive biblical truth from people who complement our learning styles. Ministry teachings can be found on many social media platforms, websites, and in smaller home church settings. As I'm writing this book, there is a worldwide pandemic, and we're all counting on our electronics to keep us connected to pretty much everything. Thank God for technology. It's never too late to invest in spending one-on-one time with a wise Bible teacher. Now, you may say, "Jaiya, everyone I'm interested in learning from wants me to pay for their online conference or one-on-one coaching. Shouldn't that be free since God gave them the gift to teach?" No, and here's why. While God freely gives people the wisdom and knowledge to build others up, the time and demand for them to do so is not free. Ministry leaders often sacrifice their time and energy away from their lives and loved ones to be kingdom builders. This will always cost a leader something. When I think of partnering with someone for spiritual growth, I'm always reminded of the "Parable of the Sower" and how it benefits us to sow into those who sow into us.

Before we complete this chapter of identity and confidence, I want to leave you with a few things to think about concerning the character of modesty.

- Where would you be spiritually if you made your heart just as beautiful as your face when you are applying your makeup?

- How much would you grow spiritually if you spent the same amount of time with God as you spend (thirty minutes, one hour, two hours+) on making yourself outwardly beautiful?

- When I leave the house, am I reflecting light or darkness?

- When I leave the house, am I reflecting the natural beauty God has given me, or am I reflecting a manufactured look of sensual beauty.

Let's pray:

Father, I thank you for the uniqueness you gave me when you created me. Guard my heart against fantasizing thoughts; prevent my heart from desiring things that make me common and materialistic. Protect my character from becoming a mouthpiece of the enemy. May we present our bodies as a living sacrifice to you by eating right, living holy, and thinking positive so that your Holy name is lifted up and glorified through us. Amen.

Master Key

"Love the Lord your God with all your heart and with all your soul and with all your mind and with all your strength. The second is equally important: 'Love your neighbor as yourself.' No other commandment is greater than this."

~ *Mark 12:30-31 NIV*

Chapter Five

LOVING YOURSELF LIKE GOD LOVES YOU

It's an Obedience Issue

Jesus makes things simple, so why do we make it so hard? God makes everything beautiful in its time. All we have to do is make a decision and agree to fully commit to walking in relationship with God. The key to learning how to love ourselves requires discipline, a discipline that no longer allows hurting ourselves by lack of sleep, pleasing others, robbing time from ourselves, or idolizing professional and personal titles such as "wife" or "best friend."

Giving God our *yes* becomes a steady commitment to discipline and transformation in all areas of life. Our obedience to God's will unlocks a level of self-love you won't find in self-help books. Don't get so comfortable with encouraging everyone else that you forget to push yourself. Don't let your social life be the reason you stopped growing spiritually. Let your spiritual growth consume your social life. We are all familiar with the Ten Commandments. Most people learn those laws in "How to be a Christian 101, but did you know there are two laws greater than the Ten? Jesus refers to them as "the Great Commandments" and makes it simple for us by breaking it down into two steps. Jesus did not say, "Would you kindly do these two tiny little things," and he does not say that doing this will make life better. He says it's a must that we do them.

The Bible is full of "it's easier said than done" moments." I'm thankful that the God we serve is a hand-holding God. It's difficult to take care of anyone effectively if we aren't our best selves spiritually, mentally, or physically. Grace, mercy, and service to others require so much spiritual and physical extraction from our bodies.

Learning How to Love

The first great commandment is that we must "love the Lord our God with all of our heart, all of our soul, all of our mind, and our strength." We turn the key to abundant happiness when we live in the posture of expectation. I've found so much joy in believing that the next day will be better than yesterday because God hits the reset button on the mercy given to us for our human errors. By loving God with our hearts, we insert ourselves in the position to receive the abundance of joy as he walks with us through our daily circumstances. Notice that I said that we have joy "while" we walk with God. We have a certain peace when we are walking with an undefeated champion, our counselor, our everlasting Father, the Prince of Peace, and the Mighty God.

Loving God with all of our hearts is only the beginning of the completeness we experience by doing just this one great commandment. It means we have an emotional connection with him. Do you know that emotion that comes over us when we are praising God for all the goodness that he blesses us with? That excitement we have when we know a particular blessing has our first and last names on it? Yes, that praise, that happiness, that joy.

Other times, we assume we are all alone and battling life's circumstances with a Swiss army knife instead of our mighty sword. God wants us to give him all of that too. After all, it is an emotion within our hearts. "All of our heart" means the good, the bad, and even that one time the enemy inserted a bad word into a conversation that had us hotter than Tabasco Sauce because we meant that part too! "All of our heart" means *all* of the situations and circumstances.

Loving God with all of our heart says, "Lord, I'm tired of holding these heavy bags filled with weight gain, divorce, bankruptcy, abortion, new age entanglements, and living in an altered state that seems to numb the truth of my circumstances, and I give it over to you." We don't have to joyfully walk through bad moments, but instead, we can rely on our God, who is always there. Loving God at all times is a muscle that requires daily training. It builds a level of confidence that covers us with faith and hope in the unseen future. The key to unlocking abundant joy is remembering God's promise that we can do everything, live the life we want to live, and come out on the other side of our struggles with God, who has given us the strength and courage to do so.

When I think of loving God with all of my soul, I think about a very popular scripture in the Bible: "Now faith is the substance of things we hope for and the evidence of the unseen." When the word evidence is used, it sounds like it's a call to wait in confirmed expectation. It's as if we have a stack of documented receipts that can confirm that God has shown up in our lives. It's the evidence that God is real. Loving God with our soul is admiring and adoring the God who built our bodies, the flowers in the grass, the moon, and our entire solar system. Something in our soul confirms that we have been created by a greater being than our natural eyes can comprehend. Part of our soul is designed specifically for God to fit in. Knowing and believing that our creator has created an open book test designed for us to win confirms that he belongs there above anything else. Our soul carries us further than our hearts can. Loving God with all of our soul creates that nonnegotiable relationship with our one true living God.

Loving God with all of our strength seems self-explanatory, but the strength implied here is more than just physical. Loving God with all of our strength looks at our actions and responses with a magnifying glass. It requires us to truthfully ask ourselves if we love our spouse and children in a way that displays love, joy, patience, kindness, gentleness, and goodness. Do others see us as living examples of self-control and faithfulness?

Worshiping God is a lifestyle of honoring God. Loving God with all of our strength means choosing right from wrong— a decision to go down the least popular path, to use our words and spiritual gifts to speak against injustices with boldness and wisdom. Loving God with all of our strength is one of the biggest faith leaps we will ever have to take because we are often leaping into unknown territory. Thankfully, we have a Father who always catches us.

Jesus answered, "Everyone who drinks this water will be thirsty again, but whoever drinks the water I give them will never thirst. Indeed, the water I give them will become in them a spring of water welling up to eternal life."
~ John 4:13-14 NIV

Proactively Loving Yourself

It's impossible to pour from an empty cup, so don't let your well run dry. I remember being in a mental space of not knowing who I was after becoming a mom. Using your body to develop human greatness is exhausting! Before meeting my husband, I thought marriage was about living with one of your favorite people for the rest of your life, with the added bonus of regular bed bouncing. Well, that is almost the truth, but not quite. We don't consider the amount of energy expended daily from being a mom, wife, daughter, friend, and mentor.

Breathing life into anything extracts energy from us. Giving birth isn't exclusive to just human birth. We give birth to new business ideas, educational efforts, careers, and so many other things. These births create labor pains and require intentional nurturing after the birth process. Through all of this, we have to remind ourselves that we serve a big God who helps us overcome tiny problems that overwhelm us. We live in a world of hustling and fast-paced living where it is easy to overlook our needs, especially if we are the ones who are needed.

How full is your cup right now? Have you been convincing yourself that you're just fine because you're used to (or even addicted to) being busy, productive, and on the edge of pure exhaustion? Refilling your well takes time. The key to unlocking our joy is finding value in letting the Word of God pour into us before we pour out into anything else. In John 4:13, Jesus says that we become an everlasting spring of water when we are in a relationship with him. He is the source of our energy.

Wouldn't it be amazing to go to a "Wellness Spa" that actually focused on lasting freedom? I never quite understood soaking in water in a secluded area under the sun only to return back home to the same bondage that you attempted to escape. True wellness is soaking in a spiritual bath of deliverance, healing and freedom. Not a temporary escape from bondage. Taking a personal inventory of everything that helped us become who we are today is an important key to unlocking our joy. This may sound silly, but taking this very small step is a very powerful component in adding water to your well. Taking inventory of our lives requires us to observe and relearn everything we love to do—things like going to the movies, window shopping at the mall, or visiting the zoo, aquarium, or museum. People who love all things creative may want to get back into painting, drawing, or sewing once a week. Paying attention to these tiny details light a fire in our spirit that begins to crank the pump to our internal well.

After praying, I decided to focus on nourishing and healing my soul. I had to get current with the times and educate myself on how much the world had grown while I was in a season solely focused on mothering. First, I needed a tool that would be flexible with my schedule, something I could pause and play when the tempo of my day began to speed up and slow down. I began listening to podcasts that poured water into my well. I subscribed to a health podcast to learn how to naturally increase my energy and the benefits of a daily schedule and fitness. I also subscribed to podcasts that taught me about managing my finances, home, and parenting, and podcasts that served as nourishment for my soul.

Podcasts allowed me to water my well while I knocked out some of my daily goals. After years of listening to podcasts and sharing a link to everything that I thought was amazing content with my husband, he decided to subscribe our family to YouTube Premium. I thought this was the best gift! No commercials, and I could listen when I was not able to sit down and watch it. I could create folders to manage all my favorite videos, tutorials, and recipes. Can we just praise God for men who believe in investing in the soul of a woman?! Yes, God.

Do What's Good for Your Soul

When we become present with our life, we start recognizing who and what our personal time robbers are, and then we can either minimize or eliminate them altogether. Personal time robbers unconsciously rob us from being focused on what God wants us to do with our lives. Social media is a time robber. It has turned into this mind-numbing addiction that we have to pull ourselves out of in order to get our spirit back into alignment. If you have to "fast" or refrain from social media for any amount of time, that is a pretty good indicator that social media is not unlocking your joy.

Our mobile devices either include or have apps that will give us a weekly report of screen time. Social media is a great way to connect to people, but one can log on and begin mindlessly scrolling and reading. Before you know it, you've been on social media for hours, like an entire shift at work. Those hours spent doing mindless scrolling can be dedicated to personal development and growth. As a writer, I enjoy the motivational and inspirational aspect of social media sharing, but I have found that creating healthy boundaries is an important key to maintaining my personal joy.

Some of us naturally have a "savior complex." A savior complex is when we feel like we have the power to save someone by exhausting personal energy to fix a problem. The key to unlocking everlasting joy is to stay in our lane by letting Jesus be Jesus. He is the savior. The longer we place ourselves in the position of Jesus, the farther we end up pushing our loved ones back from receiving the actual help that they need. We get so consumed with personal time robbers that we feel obligated to meet their needs, and if we don't, we feel like we have completely failed them as a friend. People who believe that couldn't be more wrong.

If God is not focused on pleasing everyone's demands, why do we feel obligated to? Are we better than God? We put ourselves at risk of double-sided disappointment and a decreased value in friendships. When we stop people-pleasing, there is a faith shift from us to God. We help others the most when we help and heal ourselves. When we invest in ourselves, we become the strongest motivators to get up and go. It's one thing to tell someone to "make it a great day," but why not show them how by intentionally making every day great for ourselves and sharing how we did it? I have a great example of this, and I'm sure that you can relate. Remember the friend you invited to the gym at the beginning of your fitness journey? They consistently declined until they began to see those curves getting tighter and the inches falling off. Suddenly, they call to ask about your workout schedule, and they invite themselves.

Resentment Is Killing You, Sis!

Bitterness is like a poisonous slow death. Thankfully, there is an antidote. Forgiveness. Let it go, give it to God, and get on with your life. God wants us to hand over all our emotions so he can work on them. When I was younger, my mom would always ask me, "How long are you going to beat that dead horse?" In other words, "When are you going to let that go and give that emotion to God?" I got so mad at her because I felt like I deserved and earned my little "angry minutes," but she was right. How long would I let that bad energy consume me?

Nelson Mandela once said, "Resentment is like taking poison and waiting for your enemy to die." Resentment and bitterness are poison to the spirit. They will eat away at you until you can't even recognize yourself. Everyone says lack of communication is the relationship killer, but I disagree. Although communication is very important, resentment is the killer of all relationships. The key is to allow and accept the human moments of others. Resentment keeps us from unlocking the fullness of peace and joy. We can have resentment toward another person for years; meanwhile, they moved on with their life within seconds after the issue started. Resentment won't have you running to the courthouse to draw up divorce papers; no, it is a much slower process with multiple victims, including you. Resentment poisons relationships between siblings, family members, friends, and coworkers.

The quickest way to find happiness and absolutely eliminate resentment is to forgive. Yes, we all have heard of forgiveness, but do we forgive daily or maybe even hourly like we need to? Forgiveness is our strength and gives us so much power and increases our energy level instantly. Forgiving someone will free up so much of your life. Unforgiveness and bitterness can wear us down. You never know how much energy resentment was sucking out of you until one day, you finally let it go. Forgiveness also gives us peace. Let it go and you will grow. Ephesians 4:31 says it best:

> "*Let all bitterness and wrath and anger and clamor and slander be put away from you, along with all malice. Be kind to one another, tenderhearted, forgiving one another, as God in Christ forgave you.*"

We are our first ministry, and once we are spiritually full, then we can pour into others. Unlock your joy by establishing a community of people who find joy in pouring into you and filling your cup daily.

Let's pray:

Heavenly Father, thank you for every day that you choose to breathe life into me. Help me give myself the same level of grace and acceptance you have given me. I desire to fall in love with the authenticity of me. Give me the strength to eliminate my time robbers, unhealthy thought patterns, negative emotions, and toxic behaviors. Help me serve from the wholeness I have found in you. Forgive me for any feelings of selfishness, resentment, self-condemnation, and any misinterpretation of my life experiences.

In Jesus' name, amen.

Master Key

"Put on then, as God's chosen ones, holy and beloved, compassionate hearts, kindness, humility, meekness, and patience, bearing with one another and, if one has a complaint against another, forgiving each other; as the Lord has forgiven you, so you also must forgive. And above all these put on love, which binds everything together in perfect harmony."

~ Colossians 3:12-14 ESV

Chapter Six

KINGDOM RELATIONSHIPS

Family

Have you ever noticed the dynamic between Jesus and his family? The Bible tells us that Jesus had a mother, father, and siblings—both sisters and brothers. At the age of twelve, Jesus left his family to go to his Father's house. Jesus knew he was created to make a difference at a very young age, and he was persistent in teaching everyone of all ages about God. As a young twelve-year-old, Jesus went to the temple and astonished Bible teachers with his knowledge: *"And all who heard Him were astonished at His understanding and answers"* ~ *Luke 2:47 NKJV.*

This is very important to remember when we hear children say and do profound things at early ages. When I watch our daughter make sound judgments at only three years old, I'm reminded that children are our reward from heaven. The younger they are, the closer they are to God. They just left heaven and are operating as pure souls. No media or television programming has tainted them. Luke 2 confirms that young people can teach the old and that their wisdom should not be disqualified because of their age. God gave us the authority to overcome all power over the enemy; this level of authority does not have an age limit on it. We should not let overcooked Christians and non-believers distract us from the truth. No matter the age, we all read the same Bible.

> *"Therefore let no one pass judgment on you in questions of food and drink, or with regard to a festival or a new moon or a Sabbath. These are a shadow of the things to come, but the substance belongs to Christ. Let no one disqualify you, insisting on asceticism and worship of angels, going on in detail about visions, puffed up without reason by his sensuous mind, and not holding fast to the Head, from whom the whole body, nourished and knit together through its joints and ligaments, grows with a growth that is from God."*
>
> ~ *Colossians 2:16-19 ESV*

Jesus was respectful toward his family and valued creating healthy boundaries between them. The Bible does not give anyone a pass to mistreat others. Have you ever noticed that punching someone or giving someone a good roundhouse kick to the face isn't documented in the Bible? Verbal or physical abuse was not tolerated during the ministry of Jesus Christ.

Jesus only allowed anyone to physically mistreat him when it was time to fulfill God's plan. In fact, Jesus clearly shows us how to assert our authority when being disrespected all throughout the book of John. We should never let anyone mistreat us, including those who hold titles in ministry. We are called to honor ourselves and have a level of integrity.

Creating healthy boundaries within relationships, especially in our families, allows us to love one another without compromising our spiritual maturity and growth. In a perfect world, we would love for those who know us the best to walk with us during this journey, but what if they don't? Jesus had unsupportive family members. Mary and Joseph did not know how to support Jesus' ministry, so he went out and built relationships with people who would. The sooner we respond to unsupportive people in our lives, the faster we will be able to put a boundary in place that eliminates disappointment. Mary had moments where she doubted her son, and the rest of her children had their moments when they did not believe: *"For not even his brothers believed in him"* ~ *John 7:5 ESV.*

Creating healthy boundaries allows us to love our family for who they have shown us they are. We often use the title of "Family" to determine how we deserve to be loved, which isn't always the best example of love. As we grow and mature, we create friendships that become closer than those we share DNA with. Jesus' relationship with his family shows us that family is about love and people who share mutual love and respect for each other. We can't choose the family we are born into. The Bible warns us that there may even be enemies within our own family: *"And a person's enemies will be those of his own household"* ~ *Matthew 10:36 ESV.* We do get the opportunity to discover who our true family is. Our spiritual ties come before our family ties and are not defined or determined by our race.

> *"And his mother and his brothers came, and standing outside they sent to him and called him. And a crowd was sitting around him, and they said to him, "Your mother and your brothers are outside, seeking you." And he answered them, "Who are my mother and my brothers?" And looking about at those who sat around him, he said, "Here are my mother and my brothers! For whoever does the will of God, he is my brother and sister and mother."*
> ~ *Mark 3:31-35 ESV*

When children are adopted or fostered by people who don't share the same DNA, are they loved any differently? We are adopted by God. The love of God is more than biology, and his kingdom is full of brothers and sisters who were designed to help you carry out the purpose that God has planned for your life.

I was raised in the typical American family home with my mom, dad, and brother. The relationship between my older brother and me was a great benefit to me because I got a first-hand experience of what cool looked like. I watched him have house parties, date, go to the prom, and travel the world. I observed and made mental notes of everything, hoping when I was old enough, I would be just as cool. Our family becomes the blueprint of life navigation until we are in relationship with God and understand who our kingdom Father is.

Our relationship with God expands our capacity to love. God allows us to extend mercy, grace, patience, love, and kindness toward our family as we persistently pray for their salvation and spiritual growth. We are reminded in the Book of Acts that our whole family will be saved.

And they said, *"Believe in the Lord Jesus, and you will be saved, you and your household"* ~ *Acts 16:31 CEB.*

Now it does not say that they will be saved in our lifetime, but it does give us hope that the salvation of our entire family is possible. Don't give up praying for unbelieving family members. We should not take their resistance as the final word. All things are possible for those who believe.

Jesus always loved and honored his family until his last breath. Family is about commitment and love. Family shows up and wants us to be a part of their lives just as much as we want to be a part of their lives. Family helps us grow by sharing wisdom and experience that equip us to overcome our obstacles. Family answers the phone and fights for our success as much as we do.

Let's pray:

Heavenly Father, thank you for the gift of family and friendship. I come against any plan the enemy has planned for us. Today I put my family in your hands as I create healthy boundaries that help me to faithfully avoid the things that displease you. Lord, cover those who have not met you yet so that they have an encounter with the one true living God, Jesus Christ.

Master Key

"Then the Lord God said, "It is not good that the man should be alone; I will make him a helper fit for him."
~ *Genesis 2:18 ESV*

Chapter Seven

FRIENDSHIP

W hen you read this verse at first glance, how does it sound to you? My first question was, "Well, what about the woman? Is it good for her to live alone?" If you read this verse in literal terms, it's almost as if God is say-ing that we are perfectly fine by ourselves, but *the man,* for the love of all things holy, please don't let that man be alone. Later I realized that this verse is a call for relationship, not just any relationship but a relationship that is "fit" for the journey we are called to walk in life.

The word covenant comes to mind when I think of these types of relationships. Covenant means to be in agreement. Biblically, a covenant means to be in agreement with protecting those God has placed into our lives. We are most familiar with the word covenant being used for a husband and wife, but it can also serve the same purpose in our friendships. In our journey toward know-ing and fulfilling our calling, we will meet people who will be an influential part of our growth and have the power to shape and shift our beliefs. Maturity and experience teach us that only a specific few are fit for the journey. Let's look at how Jesus man-aged relationships: *"This is my commandment, that you love one*

another as I have loved you. Greater love has no one than this,
that someone lay down his life for his friends. You are my friends
if you do what I command you"~ John 15:12-14 ESV.
Jesus Christ had twelve friends who followed him. Out of
the twelve, one betrayed him. We also know that Jesus was very
close to three friends in particular—Peter, James, and John. Understanding the character of Peter, James, and John will give us
an idea of what Genesis 2:18 is speaking of when the verse says
"a helper fit for him." We should also pay special attention to the
'If' in this verse. Jesus had conditions for whomever he called
a "friend."

> *"You are my friends if you do what I command you."*
>
> *~ John 15:14 ESV*

Jesus was not controlling. He didn't ask his friends to be his
servants; he asked his friends to share the love of God. Jesus created healthy boundaries for his relationships. It was God's plan
for Jesus to befriend Judas Iscariot, and Jesus was wise enough
to understand Judas' purpose in his life, and he created a healthy
boundary within their relationship. The Bible doesn't say that
Jesus and Judas went to the market together to spend quality
time. Much can be learned about how Jesus managed to maintain a relationship with someone who he knew had nothing but
bad intentions for his life. God sent his son Jesus Christ down to
be an example of how we are supposed to walk in this life. God
also shows us how to avoid things that can destroy us. We must
learn from and follow Christ in everything we do. His life is the
blueprint. His life is our map.

Have you ever gotten trapped in a relationship where the
person only needed you as a trashcan? Your sole purpose in their
life was for them to dump all of their trauma on you while you
said nothing in response. Later, these people eventually found
a therapist because the free therapy venting sessions with you
weren't producing any results. Meanwhile, you were left to sort

through and discard everything that just got dumped on you. God did not intend for us to be in close relationships with people who extract from us and drain us. Beware of those relationships because they are intended to rob your time; instead, invite such people to grow spiritually so they can stand up and walk on their own. Check this out: *"Let the thief no longer steal, but rather let him labor, doing honest work with his own hands, so that he may have something to share with anyone in need" ~ Ephesians 4:28 ESV.*

How do you connect with covenant relationships? I remember sitting in church looking at the back of the church program and seeing an invitation to the woman's ministry. I wrote down the dates and times of their meetings and discussed it with my husband. I had gotten to the point where I valued the community and fellowship of women whose wisdom and experience empowered me to raise the standard of the kingdom wife and mother God created me to be. Once I started attending weekly women's Bible study, I connected with women of all ages—women whose wisdom I valued, from young to old.

Covenant relationships require us to leave the comfort of our homes and may even require us to leave our "safe" friends so the Holy Spirit can guide us into a divine introduction. Covenant relationships also naturally happen when we are in alignment with God's will for our lives. When we are aligned with the will of God, people we need on our journey show up, but if we are unstable, we will miss the blessing.

Great places for this type of connection are Women's Bible study, church, small groups, and conferences. I have found connections at conferences very fruitful because I meet like-minded people. Usually, conferences connect people walking on a similar path and with similar goals. Whenever I'm in the company of someone who shares similar spiritual gifts and hobbies, I feel like I've connected with someone who truly gets me. Jesus prayed all night before he connected with the disciples, so let's do what Jesus did and follow him.

Let's pray:

Heavenly Father,

You show me how to love and how to be a consistent friend. Help me love others as myself by creating healthy boundaries that allow me to be authentic and protect me from destruction. Give me the compassion and grace to push my friends to grow in relationship with you. Thank you, Father, for giving me the blessing of true friends that are fit for the journey!

In Jesus' name, amen.

Master Key

"Again I say to you, if two of you agree on earth about anything they ask, it will be done for them by my Father in heaven."

~ *Matthew 18:19 ESV*

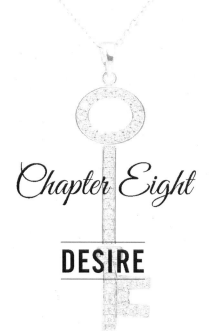

Chapter Eight

DESIRE

G od will write your love story:
Our spouses do not complete us—God does. The abundance of life God promises us will never be found in another human but through relationship with God. Our relationship with God gives us someone to turn to when we need an attitude adjustment during heated conversations. Our relationship with God provides correction when we are making wrong decisions. Between ages one and twenty-five, we experience deception, disappointment, and heartbreak from people that we trust. All of the brokenness has to heal, or it will continue to break us down, causing us to break others along the way.

Healing from life's traumas is a very important step to moving forward. Healing begins with identifying the most painful part of the process, the truth. Sometimes the truth comes from writing out our experiences in a journal. The truth can also come from spending time with a life coach, counselor, or mentor who can share wisdom as well as share biblical truth about your experiences. This kind of consistent emotional alignment will equip us to apply the same methods to every issue we will face in the future.

When we enter a marriage, we agree to love and protect that person for the rest of our lives. It's difficult to protect someone if you are a wounded warrior. Your partner needs you in the battle. Our relationship with God is the prescription for healing life's traumas before marriage. Our closeness with God has no competition. No one will ever match the covering we feel when we take all of our cares and concerns to the Lord in prayer and wait for his response.

"So you also are complete through your union with Christ, who is the head over every ruler and authority."
~ Colossians 2:10 NLT

I just knew marriage would be more like the lazy river of love and romance; instead, it's the rocking roller coaster of love. I would've loved to join the bandwagon of social media hashtags that said #IMarriedMyBestfriend, but I didn't. Not at first anyway. I did not marry my "best friend." We turned the corner into the best friend gang after year five when we realized we actually liked each other and could do this thing called marriage for life, but that is not how we began.

I remember seeing all of these couples bragging on social media about how being "married to your best friend" was relationship goals. I agree—you want to get to a point in your marriage where not only do you love your spouse but actually like them ninety percent of the time. Seeing this cliché quote on social media use to grind my gears because I believed a best friend was someone who knows you better than anyone else. They have seen you on your worst days and celebrated with you on your best days. I had a great best friend before I even knew my husband, and if he was to become my best friend, he had a lot of catching up to do. A wife should never feel pressured to agree with cliché' social media fads if that is not the fabric of their relationship.

The biggest difference between my friends and my husband is that marriage makes you one flesh (Mark 10:8). This is ten times more special than what I have with the women in my life.

Down the line, I noticed that the formula of "marrying your best friend" was never the remedy for a successful marriage. The remedy for a successful marriage is God.

"For where two or three are gathered in my name, there am I among them."

~ *Matthew 18:20 ESV*

Accountability within marriage creates trust and joins us together as one flesh. Accountability becomes a lifestyle habit and requires transparency, honesty, access, and genuine responses to questions. Love is work. We respect our managers enough to provide detailed responses at work, and our spouses deserve the same detailed communication. Choosing to hold each other mutually accountable removes the enemy's influence to hide things from your spouse. Here are some areas in marriage where accountability has to take place:

- Decisions
- Finances
- Weekly schedules
- Boundaries for relationships outside of the marriage, i.e., in-laws and extended family members
- Technology
- History
- Faithfulness
- Kindness toward each other
- Patience
- Service
- Being respectful
- Forgiveness

But when you are praying, first forgive anyone you are holding a grudge against, so that your Father in heaven will forgive your sins, too."

~ *Mark 11:25 NLT*

Unforgiveness in marriage is the devil's playground, but forgiveness equals freedom. I learned that the faster I forgive, the faster I am free from the enemy planting crazy thoughts in my head. The devil is a liar! Designate a counselor or a couple who is willing to get in the mud with you and your spouse and pray. During the heated moments, you need a couple that can speak life and truth into your marriage.

"Understand this, my dear brothers and sisters: You must all be quick to listen, slow to speak, and slow to get angry."

~ James 1:19 NLT

The enemy makes it so hard to pray for our spouse. He makes it even harder to pray with them because he knows that a married couple operating in agreement is a powerful relationship. Creating agreements within marriage work like binding contracts. Once we make these agreements with our soul, we will create new habits that align with the agreement.

The verse above states that if two or three pray together, God is in the midst. Praying together in marriage is where the real power is. It promotes unity and emotional intimacy in the relationship, and it invites God into the marriage. Our battles as married couples are never what we see in front of us. They are always unseen, so we have to attack those battles in the spiritual realm.

"I tell you the truth, whatever you forbid on earth will be forbidden in heaven, and whatever you permit on earth will be permitted in heaven."

~ Matthew 18:18 NLT

Are you ready to start praying with your spouse? Here are seven tips you can start practicing today:

- Communicate with your spouse what is on your prayer list so you can agree in faith that it will happen.
- Pick a specific time to pray together during the day.

- Don't hesitate to pray spontaneous prayers throughout the day for each other.
- Take turns praying and alternate days. When your spouse is praying, quietly listen and wait for your turn.
- You can pray together silently, but when Jesus prayed to God, he prayed out loud.
- Do not victimize or bash each other during prayer.
- Encourage and speak life into each other.

Don't just pretend to love others. Love them. Hate what is wrong. Hold tightly to what is good (Romans 12:9 NLT).

Let's pray: Singles, you can pray this one too!

Father, I'm so thankful for (insert name) and that you have made us one flesh. Show me how to love (insert name) in even greater ways than I do now. Let nothing destroy what you have joined together. Help us to be kind, loving, romantic, and passionate toward each other. Remind us to desire and prefer each other above anyone else. We pray against all fear, unhappiness, and bitterness. Our marriage will not be frustrated by a lack of finances but, instead, with an overflow of heavenly blessings. Help us to be forever united in our minds, bodies, and spirit.

In Jesus' name, amen.

ACKNOWLEDGEMENTS

To the Head of the Church, our redeemer, the one true living God, Jesus Christ, who offers us open book tests and grace upon grace. I humbly lay this work at your feet.

To My Family: My Love King, Charlon, thank you for stretching my capacity of faith and belief in the impossible and unexplainable. I'm thankful for your compassion, friendship, and kindness. Having a husband who enjoys walking faithfully alongside me is an answered prayer. My daughter Chai, thank you for taking this journey with me and Daddy. You are such an intelligently sharp little girl and you inspire me daily to let God be God. You two are with me as I hit every destination that God brings us to. You keep me focused and make this life an adventurous and joyful life to live.

Mom: Hey girl! I love you and thank you sooo much for being the type of mother that I needed. Thank you for telling me that I would be a teen mom if I ran the streets, and that I would get fired from my Job if I got too prideful, HA! Your direct, non-sugar-coated conversations formed all my life decisions and made me who I am today. I appreciate your wisdom and your commitment to our family.

Dad: Even though you are not physically here, you are such an MVP in my life. You showed me how to discern good vs. evil and how to laugh at everything because life is too short not to find moments of joy in everything.

My Kingdom Family: Debbi Butler, you caught the vision of the journey that God has me on and you responded with obedience. I have such deep gratitude for you as you walked with me through God's wisdom and truth, your discipleship has been such a privilege. So has your invaluable investment in me as a leader by sharing your time and countless conversations filled with teaching me, correcting me, and encouraging me. Thank you for picking up the phone when I called to go through my growing pains as I poured into these chapters. I'm so thankful for your consistent instruction, guidance, friendship, and for always requiring that I choose joy in the Lord

Thank you to the countless Bible teachers, pastors, intercessors, prophets, and apostles who have sharpened my perspective and understanding.

My church family: Wowww, so many to name! Just know that if I have ever sat in a Bible study, discipleship group, spiritual growth class, or simply attended the same service time as you this is for you. Thank you! I was listening and I was taking notes. **BIG HUGS**

My friends: Thank you for all your prayers, encouragement, and endless offers of help made to make this book possible.

Lastly, to every reader who made a commitment to praise our Lord in the diligent study of his word, I am humbled and honored to journey right beside you. Thank you for giving me the privilege.

ABOUT THE AUTHOR

Passionate, playful, sensational, and fearless. These are just a few words that describe Jaiya Clarke, a native of the sunny city of Orlando, Florida.

Jaiya has discovered that her life's purpose is to inspire, encourage, and equip women to discover their unique identity so they can experience God's truth no matter where they are in the world. She regularly teaches Bible studies and is passionate about discipleship. Jaiya is a military spouse and mom who now resides in San Diego, California. Connect with her at JaiyaClarke.com

CONNECT AND SHARE

If you enjoyed this book purchase copies for others you know and leave a review on Amazon.com. Author Jaiya Clarke would love to connect with you. Visit JaiyaClarke.com to stay up-to-date about the author's events and releases.

Follow @JaiyaClarke on Instagram.

Join Jaiya's next masterclass for women!

Visit JaiyaClarke.com to sign up.

"I have grown so much and learned so much from our Bible study class. You have so much knowledge that you pour into us every week. The way you explain a scripture so that beginners like me, who are new to studying the Bible can understand it and relate it to our current lives. You have been a blessing in my life, and I am forever grateful that God led me to our Bible study group "Armored Swords of Christ." My spirit is filled up after every class."

—Anji S., San Diego, CA

"From the moment I met you I could feel His presence on you and that's why I was always so comfortable around you at S.I.S.T.E.R.S even with my apprehension of being around women. Your delivery in our weekly Bible study is a blessing and helps cultivate a deeper relationship with our Lord and Savior by guiding through His word and encouraging open discussion for understanding, growth, and healing. You are truly a blessing and I'm grateful God placed you in my life!"

—Monique F., Chula Vista, CA

"The Armored Swords Bible Study group with Jaiya has been amazing. To learn with a group of women in different stages of life allows one to evolve even more in this walk of Life with Christ. We come as we are even during a pandemic through Zoom. A safe space to strengthen one another during good and tough times. It's like having supporting pillars only to keep building you up. It's something I look forward to every week. We only aspire to spread his goodness in ourselves, in our homes, and in every life we come across."

—Rachel D., San Diego, CA